The Strategic Poet

Also by Diane Lockward

The Uneaten Carrots of Atonement
Temptation by Water
What Feeds Us
Eve's Red Dress

Greatest Hits:1997 – 2010 (chapbook)
Against Perfection (chapbook)

The Practicing Poet: Writing Beyond the Basics
The Crafty Poet II: A Portable Workshop
The Crafty Poet: A Portable Workshop

The Strategic Poet

Honing the Craft

edited by

Diane Lockward

Terrapin Books

Terrapin Books
4 Midvale Avenue
West Caldwell, NJ 07006

www.terrapinbooks.com

ISBN: 978-1-947896-48-2
Library of Congress Control Number: 2021942587

First Edition

Cover art:
Feather pen with antique inkwell
by LiliGraphie

Contents

VII. Figurative Language: Metaphor

VIII. Figurative Language: Personification

IX. Figurative Language: Hyperbole

X. Figurative Language: Apostrophe

XIII. Odd Forms

Introduction

The Strategic Poet: Honing the Craft is a follow-up to my previous craft books: *The Crafty Poet: A Portable Workshop; The Crafty Poet II: A Portable Workshop;* and *The Practicing Poet: Writing Beyond the Basics.* Like those books, this one focuses on craft and emerged out of my belief that craft can be taught and that the best teacher of craft is a good poem. Like the earlier books, this one assumes a knowledgeable reader, that is, one who already knows the language of poetry and already practices the craft. It is my hope and my intention that this book will build on and hone the reader's skills.

This new book is organized into thirteen sections, each one devoted to a specific poetic strategy. My baker's dozen is admittedly somewhat arbitrary, but it's also logical as it moves from the most basic strategies to more challenging ones. While only thirteen strategies are used for organizational purposes, the reader will find many additional strategies referred to and discussed within the sections. There is a progression from one section to the next, but each section also stands alone, so the reader or teacher can follow the order of the Contents or move about freely among the sections.

Each section begins with a Craft Talk. A few of these were borrowed from my monthly Poetry Newsletter, but most were solicited specifically for this book. I reached out to poets whose mastery of craft I admired. Each Craft Talk is followed by Model Poems and Prompts. Each Model Poem is followed by an analysis of its craft elements, especially its use of the section's strategy.

One Model Poem in each section is followed by a Commentary, a feature new to this book. I invited the poet who wrote the model poem to comment on a particular strategy used in the poem. I expect that readers will enjoy the poets' commentaries on their own poems and will find them informative.

Each of the thirty-six Prompts is followed by two Sample Poems. These poems were written to the prompts and came from a Call for Submissions sent first to the subscribers of my newsletter and later posted to social media. I received many wonderful submissions from poets throughout the United States. These seventy-two poems should demonstrate that the prompts are not mere exercises and can produce terrific poems. Some of the Sample Poems adhere rather closely to the directions in the prompts; others roam more freely.

While each section of my earlier craft books ended with one Bonus Prompt, each section in this book ends with three Bonus Prompts, making a total of thirty-nine additional prompts. I solicited different poets to each contribute three prompts relevant to one of the section strategies. These short prompts are not preceded by model poems and analysis. They provide additional practice with the strategies, can be used multiple times, and should lead to some good poems.

Every once in a while, someone tells me, *I don't like prompts.* Or, *I can't write to prompts.* Or even, *Real poets don't use prompts.* And yet I've been in a number of workshops where prompt deniers produced beautiful work written to prompts. Whether you are working with this book in a writing group, in a classroom, or on your own, I ask that you give the prompts a try. If, while you're writing, you feel a tug to go off in a different direction, by all means, go there. Think of the guidelines as suggestions, not laws. Remember that as far back as Antiquity, Aristotle advocated the artistic principle of imitation and invention. That's what this book advocates.

As the sample poems illustrate, real poets do indeed write real poems from prompts. Now set about honing your poetic skills and writing your own real poems.

Diane Lockward

I. Descriptive Details

Accuracy is the gateway to mystery.

—Denise Levertov

Craft Talk: From Detail to Discovery

—Ellen Bass

E. L. Doctorow said, *Good writing is supposed to evoke sensation in the reader—not the fact that it is raining, but the feeling of being rained upon.* That is our job description. But how do we go about this work of transferring feeling? How do we write poems that make the reader feel the rain? Fortunately, one of the main ways is very concrete. We create a physical and emotional impact through vivid detail, precise description, metaphor, and image. By observing, we see more. By describing what we see, we understand more, we feel more. We discover something we didn't know before. And that process of seeing, understanding, feeling, and epiphany then takes place in the reader as well.

We don't want to simply report; we want to enact an experience. And the most basic building block is detail. Detail, to be effective, must be both sensory and necessary. Details arouse, shape, and direct the reader's experience. Every description reveals what we think, feel, see, and know. Any description says as much about the writer as it does about the thing being described. And in this way the distance between the writer and the reader collapses and intimacy is achieved.

If I could give just one suggestion to beginning and developing writers, it would be to slow down. If you don't rush through what you see or what you want to convey, you have a better shot at delivering a real and vivid experience to the reader. You might find it helpful to think about it this way. Imagine that you walked into a room where the TV was on and a movie was playing. You haven't seen the beginning; you don't know what the film is about. But if you watched just for one full minute, think about how much you'd see and hear. To write all that you observed would take many pages. You'd have to describe the terrain, the landscape, the setting, the people, their expressions, gestures, how they moved or didn't move, what they said and how they said it, how all this shifted when the camera zoomed in or panned out—and more.

You see immediately how much might possibly enter your poem just from one minute. And when we're drawing from life, either our own or others, we have all of the senses, as well as feelings and thoughts. Of course, you can't just include everything. No one is interested in a recital of unconstructed life. The writer, Janet Burroway, said, *If you refuse to direct our judgment* [through the selection and sharing of specific detail], *you may be inviting our indifference.*

Chekov defined talent as the ability to distinguish the essential from the inessential. So we are always going to be choosing *which* detail. In the early drafts of a poem, you may want to focus just on including detail and trying to make that detail as sharp as you can, erring on the side of too much detail, rather than too little.

As you develop your craft, it will be necessary to make sure those details are both relevant and necessary. They have to earn the real estate they take up in the poem. The amount of space given to them—and if they're allowed to stay at all—depends on whether and how significantly they function in the poem. If a particular detail doesn't add to the poem, then even if it's interesting in itself, it has to be asked to leave.

You may struggle with which details are essential, but by focusing on vivid, sensory detail, you'll be moving in the right direction. Because it's through details, description, images, and metaphors that we are led to understand something about the experience or the subject we're writing about that we didn't know before we began the poem.

And this discovery is at the heart of why we write at all. Because we want to discover something we didn't already know. We want to be enlarged. We want to be transformed. A good poem changes both the writer and the reader.

The novelist, John Gardner, said, *Details are proofs. They prove the existence of the world.* This practice of closely observed, precisely rendered detail will absolutely make your poems stronger. And change your life.

Poem and Prompt

Dreaming Alabama

I summon to my tongue Tuscaloosa. Opelika. Eufala.
Then Tuskegee. Wetumpka. Talladega. Swirl the muddy
tang of the swollen Coosa River. The double-named dead
of my childhood: Miss Jenny, Eva Catherine, Idonia Lee.
Hum of hymn, of the friend I have in Jesus. I roll a drawl
through bourbon and julep, drone the litany of all my blood.

I dream heavy voluptuous air, asphalt that steams
after downpour, dust swirls, dirt roads printed in toes
and hound paws. In a pick-up, I track pit stop barbeque,
ramshackle honky-tonk, river delta. To jukebox and twang,
a two-step insists, a fistfight always in the offing, sweating
bottle on a chipped bar, a man who will call me Darlin'.

I conjure wisteria. Magnolia. Spanish moss foreshadowing
sin and its jubilee. Hellfire. The Holy Ghost of Gulf
and shrimp gumbo. A Christ haunt from Dothan to
Birmingham. Through my mama's Montgomery, a march
of gospel and burning. Wings and the risen above Mobile:
Pelican. Cormorant. Impossible great blue heron.

—Melanie McCabe

McCabe's title announces that her poem will be a reimagining of the state of Alabama. She names towns and cities, choosing ones with wonderful sounds. She lists some people she knew in Alabama. She adds in lots of local color, e.g., references to the religion of the area, the drinks, food, climate, dances, music, and birds. The local color is scattered throughout the poem. In particular, notice how the motif of religion runs throughout the poem.

One of the charms of this poem is its language; keep in mind that the poet uses language that is readily available to us all if we just pay attention.

The poet uses first person and the present tense to recall the past. Notice that each stanza begins with *I* followed by a strong verb. While the poet sets up a pattern, she wisely varies it by changing the verbs at each stanza's opening.

There's pattern also in the stanza format—three stanzas, each six lines with those lines fairly even in length.

Notice syntax in this poem, the way McCabe mixes fragments and complete sentences. This mixture affects the poem's rhythm, giving it a stop-go pace, a pause and then a movement forward.

Finally, notice the ample use of alliteration: *tongue, Tuscaloosa, Tuskegee, Talladega*; the *double-named dead*; *Hum of hymn and have*; *my mama's Montgomery, march,* and *Mobile*. The wonderful diction, the pace gained from the syntax, and the alliteration make this poem a joy to read aloud.

✐ ✐ ✐

For your poem of local color, first choose a state or particular locale from your past as your subject. Then make a list of its cities and towns or locations such as lakes and parks.

Next list elements of local color: food, music, dances, animals, bugs, flowers, trees, weather. Also make a list of cool names of people who inhabited this locale. Carefully choose words for their sound value.

Begin your draft with first person and present tense. Get in strong verbs, e.g., *I remember, I recall, I go back, I call forth, I want*. As you proceed, weave in the material from your lists. Just keep going until you've used it up.

In your next draft, break your material into stanzas, each stanza the same number of lines, each beginning with *I* plus a verb.

Get a pattern working in the poem. Alternate fragments and complete sentences.

In your next draft, weave in a motif, e.g., a flower, a bird, bugs, trees.

Spruce up your diction to capitalize on alliteration.

Sample Poems

Land of the Southwind

after Melanie McCabe

I summon Fox. Kickapoo. Shawnee.
Also, Atchison. Topeka. Burnett. Entreat
the gritty Kaw. Tall figures of history:
John Brown. Carry Nation. Gordon Parks.
Adolescence accompanied by *Dust
in the Wind. Carry on My Wayward Son.*
My cot-caught merger rising above wheat, sorghum,
milo, a rural adoption in tornadic decibels.

I aspire to tumultuous atmospheres, green sky before
the hail, combines in the field, morels beneath fallen
elms. In the Chevy's bed, I stack square bales, split
wood, too. Shuffle around slurred speech that seeks
argument, past the *pfst* of a pull-tab can. That man
who used to call me *Mouse.*

I conjure milkweed. Crabapple. Columbine whispers
romance and foolishness. Victory. America's bread
basket. Dorothy's birthplace an impetus for escape.
Passage to Oregon, to Santa Fe, westward expansion
from my mother's Kansas City. Settlers dispersing like birds:
Starlings. Hawks. The incomparable Western Meadowlark.

—Lisa Haase-Jackson

Dreaming the Garden State

I imagine the landscape of Eagle Rock Reservation
overlooking the Hudson. New York City, the other side
of the river. Route 9 connecting ocean towns from Avon

to Cape May long before the secret got out. The crested
cardinal with his slurred whistles. New Jersey. Wild canary.
Blue meadow violets. Cranberry fields, blueberries,

tomatoes. Eggplant like the darkest wine in aubergine
wineskins. I call out Princeton. Paramus Blue Laws,
Monmouth thoroughbreds moving like the wind.

Rutherford, Paterson, magnolia, and peonies. Hymns
that run through my veins. Nanna's summer tapestry
of meals, *children should be seen and not heard.*

I trace the wooden Cyclone rollercoaster of the Palisades,
Votee Park's ice pond, flashes of skates, bonfires,
that first time feeling of driving my secondhand Chevy.

Murray the K's "Swinging Soiree" blasting on the radio.
I envision Atlantic City, conch shells, one-legged sandpipers,
Lucy the Elephant Hotel, the salty air of the boardwalk.

Even as the world circles, I recall Jersey, my mother of pearl.
I claim this dream winged out to sea like a cormorant
on an enormous wave as the shoreline fades.

        —Deborah Gerrish

Poem and Prompt

Old Man Wandering the Roads

My grandfather grafted trees and sold the shoots
across four counties to farmers who wanted
new fruit for canning, an apricot or yellow pear,
jar of late autumn to sweeten winter bread.

He left a trail of growing things wherever he went,
and carried a little change in his pockets
to prove he had done his day of work,
maybe not a lot of it, but enough to get around,

enough to buy gas for an old Ford, Coca-Cola
for the road, sardines and saltines for dinner.
I remember him as a talker who visited often
but never stayed long, sitting shoulders forward

on our couch, cradling an empty coffee cup,
anxious to tell where he'd been that morning,
as my father listened with his eyes cast down,
trying not to notice split seams and unlaced shoes.

Old man wandering the roads, my mother said,
clearing plates and cups once he was gone.
And each time my father went outside with him
when he left, walked him slowly to his truck,

but never came straight back into the house,
finding something always to do in the fields,
new ground ever to break, a stump to haul away,
some old animal dying and needing buried.

—Jesse Graves

This poem is a character study of someone the speaker knew but not very well. Writing in first person, the poet uses details to characterize his deceased grandfather. Rather than tell us that the man was poor, he shows us with the *split seams and unlaced shoes*, the *little change in his pockets*, and his dinner of *sardines and saltines*. From the details we know also that this was a man who worked hard and had a deep respect for the land. Note the telling line that begins the second stanza: *He left a trail of growing things wherever he went.*

Often such poems begin with *I remember*, but Graves begins with the grandfather. He opens with a declarative sentence that contains active verbs (*grafted* and *sold*) and is enlarged with several modifying phrases. The second stanza follows that same syntactic pattern. Notice that the poem consists of only five sentences with lots of clauses and modifying phrases.

There is also a good deal of enjambment from line to line and stanza to stanza. Isn't this how memory works, one idea leading to the next? It's not until the third stanza that the speaker brings in *I remember*.

Notice that there is only one line of dialogue, that spoken by the speaker's mother and suggesting that the grandfather exasperated her and aroused a touch of compassion. The father's gesture of walking outside with the grandfather each time he left and not returning to the house for a length of time reveals his love and deep concern for his lonely father.

Notice how effectively Graves ends his poem with a powerful image: *some old animal dying and needing buried*. Surely that image stands in for the grandfather.

Finally, notice the formal structure of the poem. It consists of six 4-line stanzas, all with fairly even line lengths. Thus the poet imposes order on his material.

✎ ✎ ✎

For your character study poem, choose a person for your subject. This should be someone you knew but not terribly well, someone who is now dead or gone from your life in some other way. Feel free to select a grandparent, but you might also choose another relative or a teacher or a neighbor.

Jot down some recollections of this person, e.g., what was your person's job or jobs? any idiosyncracies? clothing details? interactions with people other than you?

As you begin to draft your poem, use first person and past tense to capture a personal tone and one of regret for the past.

Bring in your character right away with a strong declarative sentence that includes clauses and modifying phrases.

Do not begin with *I remember* unless you need to do that to get started. Later you'll relocate it to the middle of the poem.

Use the descriptive details from your list to characterize your subject. Use a modest number of well-chosen details. Let those details do the work of characterizing.

As you revise, find a formal structure for your poem. Use the same number of lines in each stanza and use fairly even line lengths. Feel free to depart from this direction.

End with a related image rather than a piece of information, a statement of judgment, or a summary.

Commentary: Gathering the Details

—Jesse Graves

I have rarely started a poem with the title already in mind, but in the case of "Old Man Wandering the Roads" my mother's phrase about my grandfather was so definitive to my memory of the interaction depicted in the poem that I knew I would begin there. I wanted the poem to carry some of the specific grain of speech, and the texture of my mother's voice, which I believe contains frustration as well as sympathy. That same intention to employ the language of a time and place determined the phrasing for the concluding stanza, and especially the final line, of the poem. I chose to end the poem with the colloquial *dying and needing buried*, rather than the formal *dying and needing to be buried* or *dying and needing burial*. I wanted this poem to contain descriptive details related to both my grandfather's work and his interactions, so the names of the fruit trees he grafted felt important, as well as the images that showed both the disarray of his appearance and the complex reactions he elicited from family members.

The subject matter of "Old Man Wandering the Roads" led me into some difficult emotional terrain. Most of my poems are autobiographical and look at the real people and situations from my life. My grandfather was a complicated figure in the family, somewhat eccentric, but I did not want to focus solely on that element of his personality. I hoped readers would find some dignity in his work, even though he was not driven necessarily to make money or have nice things. My father's reaction to his own father felt important to me as a child, seeing that he loved him and was patient with him, but also felt more nuanced emotional responses like embarrassment or confusion. I hoped to find the *significant* details of the situation, the kind that reveal something from the interior or even hidden beneath the surface of an exchange. "Old Man Wandering the Roads" progressed through several drafts in search of the right combination of details and representations before arriving at the final version.

Sample Poems

Aunt Ed

Edith was nobody's aunt;
she was my Aunt Thelma's friend.
Rough as a cob, Mom said, *but
good at mending broken things,*
and I liked her, sight unseen.
She took me under her wing

that week at Cherry Grove beach,
my first time away from home,
the summer I turned seven.
Buck up, Buster, she'd bark when
sand spurs lodged between my toes,
but she helped me hunt for shells

and find rabbits in the clouds.
We played Parcheesi sometimes,
the radio turned down low.
She cried tears she didn't hide
when Gene Autry sang a song
about mountains, about spring.

I remember seeing her,
eyes closed, hands and forehead pressed
against the locked bathroom door,
softly saying Thelma's name,
till at last she drew her out,
drew her in, and held her close.

—Betsy Thorne

Nilla

I was an escape artist at age three,
shucking my shoes to climb
the picket fence and run
down the alley, my terrified
mother behind, calling my name.

Where I wandered most, though,
was into the yard next door,
where a woman named Alice
sat all day on a wooden commode
fashioned by her husband.

My most vivid memory of that time
is of Alice on her porch, the flowers
of her faded housedress fanning out
above ham-sized calves, her feet
oozing like dough out of pale slippers.

How lonely she must have been,
to relish time with a three-year-old.
If I was frightened at first of this red-
cheeked woman with shopworn hair,
she won me over like a neighborhood stray.

She kept a box of Nilla Wafers,
its yellow a bit of sunshine beside her
on the platform of her privy chair,
and plied me with cookie after cookie
so I'd stay with her for a while.

By the time I was four, we'd moved away.
I wonder if she missed me, the wanderer
who'd toddled into her yard. For my part,
Nilla Wafers ever after call to mind
the full moon of her kind, resigned face.

—Yvonne Zipter

Poem and Prompt

What You Missed That Day You Were Absent from Fourth Grade

Mrs. Nelson explained how to stand still and listen
to the wind, how to find meaning in pumping gas,

how peeling potatoes can be a form of prayer. She took
questions on how not to feel lost in the dark.

After lunch she distributed worksheets
that covered ways to remember your grandfather's

voice. Then the class discussed falling asleep
without feeling you had forgotten to do something else—

something important—and how to believe
the house you wake in is your home. This prompted

Mrs. Nelson to draw a chalkboard diagram detailing
how to chant the Psalms during cigarette breaks,

and how not to squirm for sound when your own thoughts
are all you hear; also, that you have enough.

The English lesson was that *I am*
is a complete sentence.

And just before the afternoon bell, she made the math equation
look easy. The one that proves that hundreds of questions,

and feeling cold, and all those nights spent looking
for whatever it was you lost, and one person

add up to something.

—Brad Aaron Modlin

Modlin's poem recalls the lessons of fourth grade. The first-person speaker is an adult looking back on childhood, a good strategy for capturing a sense of nostalgia. The *you* of the title is presumably another fourth grader, one who missed a day of school. This *you* is the poem's auditor. This strategy of speaking directly to another person is very useful in creating a voice.

The poem itself is a list of what was taught on the day the auditor missed school. The items are presented in chronological order. Note that time is signaled with such words as *After lunch, Then,* and *just before.*

The list includes numerous descriptive details that enable us to experience a day in Mrs. Nelson's class even though, like the auditor, we weren't there. We learn that her lessons included *peeling potatoes, ways to remember your grandfather's voice,* and *a chalkboard diagram.*

Mrs. Nelson, the teacher, made education relevant, but her lessons were not always age-appropriate, e.g., as she taught a lesson about *how to stand still and listen / to the wind,* she also taught about pumping gas. In another contradiction, she taught how to *chant the Psalms during cigarette breaks.* Such disparities between appropriate and inappropriate help to characterize Mrs. Nelson and also add humor to the poem.

🖉 🖉 🖉

For your own influential person poem, first choose a figure who exerted an influence on you when you were young. This might be a teacher, a parent, religious leader, scout leader, dance or music instructor.

Make a list of what you learned from this person. Throw in a few inappropriate lessons. Remember that it's okay to invent some of the lessons.

Using your list, begin your draft. As you write, imagine a *you,* someone to whom you are speaking your poem. This will help you establish a strong voice and a tone of intimacy.

Use first person and past tense. Write as an adult looking back on the experience of your youth.

Follow some kind of ordering plan, e.g., chronological, least to most important, lightest to darkest.

As you revise, create an appealing format.

Sample Poems

What You Missed While You Were Home Sleeping Off a Saturday Afternoon Drunk

Aunt Bess, who was nobody's aunt, said the woods
were a cathedral: I should bow my head in prayer.
I said it was hard to pray while I was walking

through the woods. Besides, I said, my father
didn't believe in God. Aunt Bess stopped.
She told me people who didn't believe in God

would go straight to Hell when they died.
I said my father didn't believe in Hell, either.
He thought all of it was an elaborate scheme

to keep control over the masses. Aunt Bess said
that was blasphemy. God could strike blasphemers
dead, right on the spot. I said my father might die

from drinking or smoking too much, but God
would have nothing to do with it. We passed
the small waterfall. Aunt Bess said it seemed pure,

but it was filled with microbes that could make
anyone who drank it deathly ill. Some people
might seem pure as the driven snow, she said,

but could be filled with evil. Did I understand
the comparison? I said the woods were the woods
not a cathedral, and if my father ever found out

she'd said he was going straight to Hell, he'd laugh.
You would have, right? That throaty laugh I loved
that came from too much drink and smoke. You'd say

not to pay too much heed to a poor old woman
who had nothing to love but cats. You'd say
she was already in Hell, she just needed company.

—Lynne Knight

How Your Favorite Aunt Made Spring
Your Favorite Season

*after Brad Aaron Modlin's "What You Missed
That Day You Were Absent from Fourth Grade"*

Because one May Saturday you told
Tressie Iola, your mother's most beautiful
sister with the country bumpkin name
but the glamorous cinnamon-beige skin
and hazel eyes, how you couldn't wait to grow up
and get married and have kids,

and that same Tressie Iola, who told
your nine-year-old self how to blot
lipstick with tissue to make it last longer
even though you weren't allowed to wear it
for the next seven years, and described her most favorite,
effervescent New Year's Eve champagne
even though your parents didn't drink,

looked at you with those flashing
copper-green eyes over her frothy cup
of some multisyllabic Italian coffee and told you
with the hard-earned wisdom of a woman
who turned down a modeling career that would have
taken her to New York City and Milan
to be a wife and mother in Detroit,
Girl, one thing there will always be plenty of is sperm.
Put that stuff on the back burner and go live your life.

And every spring after that,
when the dandelion blooms danced
and white petal arabesques of apple blossoms
and green maple tree seedlings
filled and fell from the sky
like a botanical version of Magritte's
bowler-hatted raining men,
you delighted in their flight but waved them on
and wished them and all the plentiful sperm
of the world happy travels

because you were not waiting for them
to fill you with magic,
because you were living your life and learning
that you are your own magic.

—Shayla Hawkins

Bonus Prompts: Descriptive Details

—Lance Larsen

1. One Thing and Another

I once had a student, Eliza Broadbent, who wrote about trying to forget a painful breakup while dissecting a sheep brain. In these sample lines, she is and isn't talking about her own grief:

> Use latex gloves.
> Use tweezers to grab the hairlike strand of cranial nerve
>   VII on the ventral brain stem.
> Use ventilated rooms to keep from gagging on formaldehyde.
> Use the trash icon for his number and texts.
> Use your finger to peel off dura mater.
> Use concealer.
> Use sagittal cuts.
> Use a cookie tray to catch the brain juice.
> Use your scientific objectivity.
> This brain is no longer a sheep chewing long grass.
> The music of his hand on your thigh was just the opening
>   and shutting of ion channels.

Write a poem about a painful experience using technical vocabulary from an unrelated field.

2. The Legal Theft

Write a cento, a poem made up entirely of lines pilfered from other poets. Before you begin, select a title that suggests a crucial turning point, something like, "Things I Saw on the Way to My Mother's Viewing." Now steal descriptive lines from poems you admire, imagining how they might comment obliquely on the situation at hand. *Ah—but the rainbow is loud* (Elaine Equi). *I Want to turn like a mobile in a new fresh air!* (Kenneth Koch). *The rain is full of ghosts tonight* (Edna St. Vincent Millay). *The snowmen, weeping, in the green hayfield* (Olav H. Hauge). *Aisles full of husbands! Wives in the avocados, babies in the tomatoes!* (Allen Ginsberg). *The moon swung bare on its black cord over the house* (Carolyn Forché).

3. List Poem

Write a list poem, enumerating all the things you might find in a junk drawer, a taxidermy shop, a purse, a glove compartment, an alley, or a personal effects bag. Let the descriptions tell a larger story or introduce a tension associated with the speaker of the poem.

II. Diction

Poetry is a deal of joy and pain and wonder,
with a dash of the dictionary.

—Khalil Gibran

Craft Talk: Veering Your Diction

—W. Todd Kaneko

Diction is easy to take for granted in a poem, partly because so many of our word choices are constrained by our vocabularies, and partly because there's often so much else to notice in a poem—metaphor, imagery, lineation, form, and so on. It's tempting to say, *The diction is conversational* or *The diction is formal*, and leave it at that, when in reality, diction isn't necessarily a fixed characteristic in a text. Often, the way diction moves and fluctuates is crucial to a poem's workings.

For example, a poet's diction does a lot of work to create the speaker's voice. In "Hulk Smash!" Greg Santos adopts the persona of Marvel Comics' Incredible Hulk, the irradiated, green monster who mindlessly pulverizes his way through the bad guys who make him mad. In the poem, Hulk is a simple guy who, frustrated with his life, complains about his job and co-workers in mostly conversational diction. He refers to himself in the third person as the character does in the comic books, which not only creates repetition throughout the poem, but also marks how the poem veers into a low diction that enhances Hulk's simple nature.

If diction works to create character, then it might be helpful to see how a poem uses word choice for character nuance. Although the language in "Hulk Smash!" is simple, certain words like *beachcomber* and *self-reliant* and *carcasses* veer from that to reveal the intelligence beneath Hulk's childish exterior. Hulk calls himself a *regular Joe*, a slang term used by blue collar guys to describe blue collar guys. His tie is *snappy*, as opposed to *chic* or *stylish*, a word choice that displays what is perhaps a cruder understanding of what's fashionable. And calling Captain America a *douche bag* is a moment in the poem where the diction veers away from the low middle diction that has been established as the poem's normal register and into a moment of mild vulgarity. It's a quick, unexpected break that might be funny, might be offensive, and is definitely a moment where the poem's diction veers to reveal a specific side of Hulk's personality.

A similar kind of movement happens in the poem "Good Bones" by Maggie Smith, in which a mother contemplates how dangerous the world is for her children. The speaker starts in a diction that is clever and poetic, using repetition and the phrase *delicious, ill-advised things* to describe the secrets she keeps from her children. Those two words—*delicious* and *ill-advised*—are a fun pairing of the diction of a cookbook with that of a prom chaperone. And Smith uses the neutral word *children*, as opposed to any number of alternate choices. *Kids* is more informal, *spawn* more scientific, *offspring* more technical, *progeny* more formal, and no one really uses the term *fruit of my loins* except to embarrass said children at parties. The speaker at the beginning of "Good Bones" is a clever wordsmith who plays with language as a means of writing a poem about being a parent.

By the end of the poem, however, the clever, playful diction has given way to a more cynical, less confident voice. The language of poetry is replaced by the language of real estate, and then interrupted by vulgarity, a single swear word near the end of the poem. This break from the established poetic diction shows a shaken confidence in both the speaker's poetry and parenting abilities. And notice how the poem moves from *delicious*, which connotes eating and consumption, to the gross vulgarity—*shithole*—which denotes a terrible place to live, but also connotes defecation and waste. Sure, the word is vulgar, but it's precisely the right vulgar word for this particular moment in this particular poem. In that moment, the speaker senses her failure in both poetry and parenthood, punctuated by this crude word that is decidedly neither poetic nor parental.

Writing poems is as much about heightened attention to language as anything and diction is a crucial way of approaching this. Diction is a tool, not a static feature because word choice is subject to change depending on the poet's needs at any point in a poem. And as you begin to see opportunities to veer your diction one way or the other, to establish and disrupt a poem's diction, you open yourself to new ways of creating and discovering meaning in your poems.

Poem and Prompt

Entreaty

Dear spring, commit. Burst
your bee-and-bloom, your blaze
of blue, get heady, get frocked,
get spun. Enough with your tentative
little breaths, your one-day-daffodils/
one-day-dewfrost. Honeysuckle us
right to our knees. Wake us
with your all-night mockingbirds,
your rowdy tree frogs. Gust
and dust us. Pollen-bomb the Hondas
and front halls, but please, no more
of this considering. This delicate-
tendrilling. Your pale green
worries me. Your barely-tuliped
branches, your slim shoots
any sideways look could doom.
The truth is I don't want to think
about fragility anymore. I can't
handle a blown-glass season,
every grass blade and dogwood
so wreckable. I'm trying hard
to teach the infallibility
of nightlights, to ignore the revving
of my own fallible heart. Spring,
you're not helping. Go all in.
Throw your white blossoms
into my gutters. Flood
my garage, mud my suede shoes,
leave me afternoon-streaked
and sweating. Vine yourself
around me. Hold me
to you. Tighter.

—Catherine Pierce

This poem uses apostrophe as it makes a direct address to *spring*, something that is not living or able to respond. The speaker continues to speak to spring throughout the poem, making various requests of the season which, to the speaker's mind, is arriving too slowly.

The most delightful aspect of this delightful poem is its playful and extravagant diction. Note, first of all, that Pierce uses the language of spring, e.g., we find *daffodils, frogs, mud, tulips,* and *honeysuckle*.

The poet uses alliteration throughout, e.g., *Burst, blaze,* and *blue; suede shoes, slim shoots,* and *sideway; Hondas* and *halls*. She sometimes uses pairs of alliterative words separated by a conjunction or a preposition as in *bee-and-bloom* and *blaze of blue* and *afternoon-streaked and sweating*.

Notice the invented phrases: *Pollen-bomb, delicate-tendrilling, barely-tuliped branches, blown-glass season*. We even get some nicely balanced three-word inventions such as *one-day-daffodils / one-day-dewfrost*. The poet relies on the hyphen for such inventions.

And notice the inventive use of nouns as verbs: *Honeysuckle us / right to our knees, mud my suede shoes,* and *Vine yourself around me*.

This is a poem that speaks loudly with its imperative sentences, such as *Throw your white blossoms, Burst your bee-and-bloom,* and *Go all in*. These imperative sentences give the poem a voice that's forceful and bossy, cajoling and pleading.

✎ ✎ ✎

For your own poem, choose one of the other three seasons to address or choose some aspect of Nature, e.g., the ocean, a cloud, rain, irises.

Before you begin your draft, make a list of at least ten words associated with your subject. Consult a dictionary or Wikipedia if needed. You will employ these words in your poem.

Begin with apostrophe, directly addressing the subject of your choice. Sustain that throughout your poem.

Employ some of the language devices used by Pierce. Use some alliteration. Bring in some alliterative pairs.

Use some of the nouns in your word list as verbs.

Invent some hyphenated words. Bonus points for three-word combinations.

Use imperative sentences. This will give your poem a strong voice.

Sample Poems

Dear October,

Once again you fall into scent of tea olive,
reluctant to leave summer. Are you

besotted with the season of riotous love,
stuck on the summer equinox?

You the 10th month, a misnomer,
due to your Old English, Old French roots,

another sign of love no doubt, as you journey
through your beer-brewer-season—

froth me with your brew, wrap me in your Octo-arms.
Color me liquefaction in sugar maple leaves.

Apple-feed me—McIntosh, Golden Delicious,
Rome & Gala—pecan me with your crack-a-nut season

Slurp me with oysters, passion in the morning fog.
O, au-to-mal light, bent toward decline.

O you, so close to death, a breath away,
mums already a touch of November-umber,

the bard's *bare ruined trees*, Day of the Dead hovering.
Speed along, wind-whip your days,

you past middle age & while snow's not on the rooftop—
do not evening us until you fling

away *mists and mellow fruitfulness*
and hand over your cool, sweet cider.

—Libby Bernardin

Aesthetics of the Sublime

Dearest ocean
stay as you were
stop warming
stop rising
resist statistical
spoil of oil spill
reverse course of biodiverse
in decline, unbleach
your Barrier Reef, fluoresce
our fading foot- and pawprints
on the beach, lull us back
to your pure aquatic, pre-
mercury and calcium leach
age of acidification's unfathomable
brink. Don't shipwreck to surge,
to invertebrate and shell dissolve.
Don't abandon to landlocked
these moon-lonely nights.
Release your currents
from crisis, the sad sibilance
of *the sea around us.*
Be memory. Be body map.
Raise mountains. Cut canyons.
I could swim forever in your hidden.
Pacific my arms.
Atlantic my legs.
Indian my hair.
Southern my skin.
Arctic my lungs.
Be my limitless tidal.
I promise not to mine
your depths for rumored gold.
Please know that without you,
my heart is ice-break, divided,
lacks mystery, never wholly existed.
Dearest ocean, I live inland
among evergreens, staggering hillsides
of ridges and ledges. But I miss

your sublime. In another life
I was one of your waves traveling
hundreds of miles an hour toward infinity.
I've painted my walls aquamarine.
I've worn your coral.
I've swallowed your salt.
I've come up for air.

—Kate Sontag

Poem and Prompt

Respair

Every six minutes another word
is dropped from the lexicon.

Who says there's no use anymore for *woolfell,*
the skin of a sheep still attached to the fleece?

And when did we stop calling tomatoes *love apples*?
I need somewhere in the world for there still to be

a *fishwife* who understands the economy of flesh
grown taut under shimmer-skin laid out in open air.

Call me a sentimental fool, or better yet a *mooncalf,*
but I already miss the ten words that went extinct

in the last hour—before I learned their names
or tried to say something smart to make you love me.

Piepowder, drysalter, slugabed, forgotten
like the names of the enlisted in the army of Alexander the Great.

And where have they gone? Gathered on shrinking ice
with other victims of our inattention, floating out into a rising sea?

Like the last day my grandfather remembered my mother's name.
So don't mind me in the bathtub on my hands and knees

trying to keep my grandpa's mind, a polar bear,
and the word *poltroon* from spinning down the drain.

It's been left to me to save everything by remembering.
Before the cock crowed, Peter *thrice* denied Christ and

20 words marched off into the dark, never to be uttered again.
Fortunately, that night, we retained *dumbass* and *forgiven,*

two words it would be hard to live without these days.
And if I could, I'd turn myself inside out to resurrect

respair, that forgotten Emmaus Road word for
the return of hope after a long period of desolation.

—Craig van Rooyen

Van Rooyen precedes his poem with an epigraph which is the piece of information that presumably set the poem in motion. The poet then builds his poem around ten words no longer in the lexicon. Diction in a poem always matters, but here diction *is* the poem.

The first stanza's extinct word is followed by its meaning. This stanza also includes the first of four questions asked in the poem. This initial question gets the poet's mind working and pulls in the reader. Like each of the subsequent questions, it also propels the poem forward. With the first extinct word and the question, the poet has built a launching pad.

Notice that the poem takes on substance as it progresses from sheep's wool to war, to changing climate, old age, and religion. Notice too that the examples given move from impersonal to personal. We move from Alexander the Great to the speaker's grandfather and his loss of language. Notice how the biblical allusion to Peter's denial of Christ is carried out to the Emmaus Road, which according to the New Testament was the road Jesus walked after his resurrection; the poet then moves to the resurrection of the word *respair*, the return of hope.

In the fifth stanza an auditor is introduced as the speaker tries *to say something smart to make you love me*. We are not sure if this *you* is the general *you*, meaning the reader, or if it's a beloved. Either way, the poem opens and brings us in.

With a delightful touch of serious humor, the poet slips in two words that have not gone extinct—*dumbass* and *forgiven*—words we need today. The poet then ends with the word *respair*, the one we need most today: *the return of hope after a long period of desolation.* This word gains more importance than the others by its placement in the title position and at the very end of the poem.

✐ ✐ ✐

For your lexicon poem, first google "obsolete words" or "extinct words." Compile a list of a dozen such words for your poem.

Now google "quotations about words." Select a quotation about words to inspire your poem. Use it as your epigraph or work it into your poem.

To get your draft underway, start with a question that relates to your first word. Pick up with your next word. Let each new word lead to a new thought. As the poem progresses, work in two or three more questions. Let the images and thoughts take on increasing substance.

Include some allusions: a historical allusion, a biblical allusion, a reference to current events. Include some personal references.

As you move to your next draft, get your poem organized into a sensible format. You might try for one stanza per word, but feel free to stray from this as van Rooyen does. Feel free also to use up several words in a short list somewhere in your poem.

Commentary: Finding the Words

—Craig van Rooyen

Since voice creates the relationship between writer and reader, diction choices open possibility. Do you want to have a chat with the reader? Do you want to confide? Do you want to tease? Diction is your tool in creating this relationship and helping the reader feel the connection before understanding the subject of the poem. I will follow a poet anywhere she wants to lead me if the voice of the poem is interesting. To get past the first few lines, I need to feel like the writer is considering me and seeking some sort of relationship. Diction is one way for the poet to signal that consideration.

Diction also affects what a poem says, not just how it says it. In other words, voice is generative. What would it feel like to write a hymn about your divorce instead of a country song? What would it feel like to chat with the reader about your father's illness instead of describing it spiritually with an assumed *poetic* voice? In your chat, you may end up putting in something about the rerun of "Gunsmoke" playing on your dad's hospital room TV and that may lead to a memory about the toy Colt .45 he gave you for Christmas when you were six. Later revisions can amplify discoveries made in earlier drafts. We can't choose those discoveries ahead of time, but we can choose a voice that may lead us places we hadn't considered going.

"Respair" started as an obsession with archaic, obsolete words. An obsession, while useful, can only get a poet so far. What could I give a reader that couldn't be had by dipping into the unabridged Oxford English Dictionary? The word lists I started with, and that had seemed so evocative, remained dead on the page. They wouldn't come alive unless I took a stance, until I treated them in a certain way. Part of that stance involved diction choices. I didn't know I was making a choice about diction, but I knew sounding like a professor would kill the life in the poem. As I tried to communicate the sense of loss and nostalgia the old words triggered in me, I started off sounding nerdish and sentimental. Then, unconsciously, I started emphasizing that voice to see where it would lead (and to avoid sounding dry). It seemed interesting in a quirky way to use the old words casually and to begin to reveal and make fun of myself at the same time—trying *to say something smart to make you love me.* But what was the poem telling me about my obsession with words that have lost their meaning? Behind that obsession, I realized, was a sense of loss of control, and also regret. Time passes. People stop recognizing their loved ones. The planet warms. The familiar becomes unfamiliar—in part because of forces beyond our control and in part because of our own bad decisions.

Remembering the story of Peter's denial of Christ created the turn, but also presented a potential trap. The only thing worse than sounding like a teacher in a poem is sounding like a preacher. Writing against the temptation to present a moral lesson led me to *dumbass* and the meaning of *respair*. In other words, a subconscious diction choice helped me dodge the teaching moment and suggested a way to open up the poem at the end instead of resolving it.

Sample Poems

Tartle

to hesitate when introducing a person
because the name escapes memory

I can't coax her name from my floating memory—
it's a quest as futile as Don Quixote's windmill assault,
lance impotent against the circling sails.
So we stand, my friend and I, facing a woman I used to know,
even liked, and her name is stopped in my throat like a chokeberry,
a piston frozen in its pump.
                              Wind soughs through the pines,
icier as we stand and stare: my sluggish brain lost
in a chain of remembrances, chasing each synapse on its rabbit track
to find the right name, the thrill of Dickinson's wide sky a testament
to past and present kaleidoscoping—oh, why can I remember *that* name
and not *this* one? Here the connection clicks. Finally the word forms,
leaves the tip of my tongue to hum the air between us.

—KB Ballentine

Meet Me at the Growlery

A word is dead / When it is said, / Some say.
I say it just / Begins to live / That day.
    —Emily Dickinson

Then let us say them to stay them,
that we might *deliciate*—
luxuriate as we corral

these words from extinction,
scraping them together,
a *crinkum-crankum* of fancy detail.

Perhaps I'm just an old *gammer*
who craves my own *growlery*,
a stout haven for bad moods,

but Emily, could you join me there?
To savor the gloaming,
now at *twitter-light*, we could wonder

who secreted those words into hiding
when they might honey our days
with whimsy and *jargogle*?

We'll laugh at the bluebird on my phone,
all the *beef-witted* bores, their
hoddy-peak tweets.

I'll *buss* your cheek, bring you to speed,
share the world's *puckfyst*,
its thirst for your words.

We will sip tea, binge and *brannigan*
on vocabulary, nibble on sweets and yes—
leave a small bit, a *tittynope*, for the birds.

    —Lucy Griffith

Poem and Prompt

The Word *Swagger*

Swagger is a nice word, most
especially when there is a deficit of swagger.
Swagger is what you crave,
like the full tilt grit of Janis Joplin,
or the guttural smolder of James Brown.
Swagger is a flood of Elvis lookalikes
in Las Vegas—it's that glitzy, that raw.
Swagger is a mouth harp, a fiddle,
it's Ginger Baker in a bluegrass band.
Swagger is getting back your bite
like Jerry Lee after the world
has kicked you in the teeth.
Swagger is a nice word after *good,*
but swagger is even nicer after *bad.*
Swagger is what you have left
when the world has nothing left to give.
Swagger is a bray without a mule.

—George Drew

The poet has selected a noun in contemporary usage as the subject of his poem. He titles his poem with that word and then sets about defining it via examples and comparisons.

Note the syntax of the poem. Every sentence begins with *Swagger is.* This kind of parallelism is called *anaphora.* The repetition of the same words at the beginning of several sentences or phrases creates a rhythm, a kind of drumbeat, almost mesmerizing in its effect. The technique also draws attention to what follows each repetition.

Rather than provide a dictionary definition, which would not be very poetic, the poet, after asserting that there's a deficit of swagger, gives us several intriguing examples of what swagger is: it's *what you crave*, it's a *mouth harp, a fiddle*, it's *what you have left / when the world has nothing left to give*. Notice how many of the examples are drawn from the field of music: *The full tilt grit of Janis Joplin, the guttural smolder of James Brown*, and *Ginger Baker in a bluegrass band*.

The examples of swagger are often metaphorical, e.g., *Swagger is a mouth harp, Swagger is a flood of Elvis lookalikes*, and *Swagger is getting back your bite*. Note especially the metaphor that closes the poem: *Swagger is a bray without a mule*. The poet saved the best for last.

Notice too what Drew does with sounds. He gives us alliteration in *Janis Joplin, bluegrass band*, and *back your bite*. He gives us assonance in the long *i*'s of *nice, bite, like, lookalikes*. And in the soft *i*'s of *deficit, tilt, grit, fiddle*, and *kicked*.

🖉 🖉 🖉

For your own definition poem, select a contemporary noun as your subject. Let that be your title, but feel free to change it later. Perhaps *glitz, pride, audacity, poverty, mask, distance*.

Now quickly freewrite a long list of examples that illustrate your word. Give yourself ten minutes for this. Don't worry about what's good or bad. Just compile the list.

Now go over the list. Do you notice that a number of your examples come from a single field, e.g., food, clothing, weather? Exploit that field by generating a few more examples. Make some of your examples into metaphors.

Arrange the examples in a first draft. Incorporate anaphora. You might also use *is* and stick to the present tense, but you might instead switch to past tense *was*. Or you might choose a different verb, a different phrasing.

Close your poem with a strong metaphor. Save the best for last.

Sample Poems

Moxie

is a word I love to say
because it's
what I've always wanted,
in spades, in endless loops.

Moxie.

Like ripping up an insulting note
and tossing it with
a finger raised, into the trash.

Like giving a nun some lip,
jumping the turnstile
to catch the last train,

having enough spunk, sass, attitude
to contradict the judge,
push the cop, slap the dictator,

enough bravery to drink
the bitter syrup in one gulp.
When you've got Moxie,

you need black lipstick
and the purple hair to match.
You need the fur boot and

the feathered boa,
everything out of nothing.
Janis Joplin belting out

"Get It While You Can."
Without it, we are
burned-out firecrackers.

It's the *s* in savvy,
the *c* in chops,
the spots on a cheetah,

the fins on a shark,
a howl with a wolf inside.
It's a motorcycle leaping the gorge.

Without it, we are
spineless. We're pale mice
pinned to the subway tracks.

—Geraldine Connolly

At Least 17 Definitions

The soul of a violin is not its tragic,
wavering four-octave A, but a small
wooden peg between front and back
that ensures they vibrate in unison.

Soul is what's missing when I read
five columns of the tiny print
Oxford English Dictionary, the one
with its own magnifying glass,
and there's not a mention of black
or music or food. That's 1971 for you.

One root means *coming from the sea*,
like all life. In Africa, the Fang people
believed it's the eye's shiny middlespot.

Soul is the angel living in the cracks
between Aaron Neville notes. Who
can sing the restoreth my of it, the dark
night of it, the bless your little of it?

The soul to search, to keep, the old and train
of it, on ice and eater of it, the actuating
cause of an individual life of it—damn my.

The ultimate etymology is uncertain.
Perhaps an early woman gnarled
her mouth in the shape of denial,
which became what-was-just-here-
at-the-deathbed, gone in a moment.

—Tina Kelley

Bonus Prompts: Diction

—Caitlin Doyle

1. Diction as Attitude

One of the key roles that diction plays in a poem is to convey the speaker's attitude about the subject matter. Draft a poem in which the speaker describes another person. Let the description reveal the speaker's positive feelings toward that person. The other person might be a romantic partner, family member, friend, or coworker. Though you want to communicate that the speaker's overall attitude toward this person is positive, include one negative element.

Now draft another version of the poem with the same speaker describing the same person. However, this time, when the speaker describes the other person, you should convey negative feelings toward that individual. Communicate that the speaker's overall attitude toward the other person is negative, but include one positive element.

2. Playing with Levels of Language

Make a quick list of slang phrases, colloquialisms, and idiomatic language. Now draft a poem about an unusual encounter, real or imagined, in a public space. Use at least three slang words, phrases, or expressions from your list. They don't have to be related. You might incorporate the language into the speaker's voice, or you might feature spoken dialogue in the poem, or you might take some other approach. Using the language from your list may spur you to write the entire poem in similar language, or you may find that you enjoy playing with a contrast between colloquial language and more formal language.

3. Five-Dollar Words

You may be familiar with the following famous statement by Mark Twain: *Don't use a five-dollar word when a fifty-cent word would do.* Your goal with this prompt is to toss off Twain's advice and write a poem with as many five-dollar words as you can manage. Choose a subject that calls for the use of formal diction, e.g., an elegant dinner party, an awards ceremony, a eulogy, a retirement speech. What kind of speaker might use such language? Now write a poem that features elevated diction not found in everyday speech, that is, five-dollar words.

III. Imagery

Poetry is the impish attempt
to paint the color of the wind.

—Maxwell Bodenheim

Craft Talk: Four Hills and a Cloud

—Lauren Camp

Wallace Stevens began his poem "Of the Surface of Things" with this image: *In my room, the world is beyond my understanding; / But when I walk I see that it consists of three or four / hills and a cloud.*

I am a visual thinker. I came to poetry from a long career as an artist. For years, I had created pieces by manipulating color, pattern, and texture. When I shifted into poetry, I continued that practice, which meant the words had to hold those same elements for me. Imagery is one of the great gifts you can give readers—an enlarged, and sometimes surprising, lens through which they can see.

The other day I was out hiking, looking across open space to the mountains. Their silhouettes were various shades of gray and blue in the distance, their shapes and colorations illuminated by the time of day and the atmosphere that lay between ranges. And above, of course, clouds. I live in New Mexico where the cloud formations are never simply clouds. They can be puffy or effervescent or a million other possibilities. They are often fairy tale clouds, wandering above the dusty world.

As writers, we often return to the same few subjects. I don't see a problem with that. The issue is how to write about those things in new ways. One answer is to push in deeper, to defamiliarize, to introduce a tension between yourself and the subject that you hadn't formulated when you started.

Later in that same poem, Stevens defines his view: *The gold tree is blue, / The singer has pulled his cloak over his head. / The moon is in the folds of the cloak.*

Line by line, Stevens has renewed the vista for me. Next time I see the moon low on the horizon, I might see it swaddled in the singer's cloak.

In looking at a draft you've written, circle or underline the phrases that seem ordinary. You know the ones—the ready-made descriptions you didn't even have to think about. That's your task, right there, finding a way to get those images to swerve into something even you didn't expect.

I like my language to have some friction or risk—just enough to make it strange, but not so much to dismantle the image. This is a process that works best by chance. You might find those good descriptions when you're resting from the poem and busy in whatever other interests claim you—baking, gardening, science experiments, automotive repair, folding laundry, listening to podcasts, and so on. A very different subject matter might even introduce the metaphor you didn't know you were seeking.

Or you might have to build that new description, bit by bit. Focus—but loosely. When I want to shift the language I've used for an image, I sometimes scan magazine articles or nonfiction texts for individual words, holding the intention I'm after gently in my mind. I call this *word shopping*. Keep an ear open for a wondrous word or two. Might it work to replace the boring way you had written that phrase?

Mark Doty, in his remarkable poem "A Display of Mackerel," describes abalone as *the wildly rainbowed / mirror of a soapbubble sphere*, and Brenda Shaughnessy, in "No Traveler Returns," describes the self as *a sealed plastic bag of water filters floating on the sea*. Deborah Digges, in "Becoming a Poet," describes a broken wristwatch as *moon glass . . . the naked face, the brittle golden hands*.

I could pull hundreds of examples, but in just these three, you see how astounding an image can be. Your goal is to move beyond the perfectly normal mind. Send your critic off elsewhere. This is playtime. And it could take some time—so relax into it.

You can write about anything so long as you make magic in your words.

Poem and Prompt

Learned at Last Night's Lecture on Dementia

My mother's brain, ink-dark
with dying cells, pocked with holes.
We say someone's not firing on all cylinders,
not knowing it's true, that sick cells
fire, don't fire, don't fire, fire,
launch messages. into.   the dark

    spaces.
where. memory. once

                      lived.

I've found shells on the beach
riddled with pin-sized punctures,
maple leaves reduced to lace skeletons.
It's not that what's missing
had no importance.
Only that there's beauty still
in what remains.

           —Pam Baggett

Baggett gives her poem a functional title that identifies setting, time, and occasion. Such an economical move makes it unnecessary for the poet to include that information in the poem. She can instead jump right into the subject of the poem, the speaker's mother's dementia.

In this poem of empathy, Baggett's first-person speaker talks about someone else's loss, but it's a loss that also affects her because it happens to someone she loves. The speaker begins with two well-chosen descriptive details that give us an image of the damaged brain: *ink-dark* and *pocked with holes*.

In line 3 the poet uses a cliché—*not firing on all cylinders*. The cliché is redeemed as it's so accurate, a point nicely illustrated by the functionality of punctuation and spacing. The repetitions in line 5 mirror the brain not firing on all cylinders. The fractured sentence in line 6 also parallels the action of the broken brain, as does the entire second stanza with its staggered lines. Notice also the additional and unnecessary line space between lines 2 and 3 in stanza 2.

In stanza 3 the poet offers two images that beautifully mirror the brain of the speaker's mother—shells with *pin-sized punctures* and *maple leaves reduced to lace skeletons*. How accurate and lovely these images are. They work like metaphors, telling us what the damaged brain looks like. Baggett uses these images to arrive at her conclusion, the kind of conclusion that we're often (and wisely) advised to avoid in favor of ending with an image. Somehow, though, it works for the poem, and we feel satisfied knowing *that there's beauty still / in what remains*.

✎ ✎ ✎

For your own poem, select an illness or injury suffered by someone you know, someone you care about. You might begin with the x-ray image of a cancerous breast, a tooth before a root canal, or a child's broken bone, or perhaps the images from a bone density test for a person with osteoporosis, or perhaps the world as seen through cataracts.

Give your poem a title that includes setting, time, and occasion.

Use a first-person speaker who is not the person with the problem but rather someone somehow connected to that person.

Begin with descriptive details, just a few carefully chosen ones.

As your draft progresses, bring in some images that convey pictures and feelings. These images should not be part of the illness but should work as metaphors.

Commit a violation by ending with information or a conclusion rather than an image.

During revision make your punctuation, spacing, and sentence structure functional, somehow mirroring your subject.

Use some functional repetition.

If the information ending doesn't work well for your poem, feel free to adjust that.

Sample Poems

Dad's Last ER Visit

Cortical atrophy, says the ER doc
meaning atoms and molecules

are missing

seasons, skies,
constellations are cratering
as his brain retreats
like a galaxy
into its own black hole
like a child into fitful sleep.

I watch

as each thought   gasps
and flops   like a fish
out of water   he mouths
the silent air   not for air
but for   words

Move closer, stray light flickers
in his eyes. Lips move towards a name
he called you when you were young
and the night sky shone bright
in a forever kind of way.
That was long ago.
That was then
& far away.

—Jemshed Khan

Weeks Waiting for Her Release

Quiet in my bottom bunk, I listen to my uncle's
city accent. He is on the phone explaining I will
be late to half-day kindergarten—my mother's Dodge
Coronet had been struck by a semi-truck, she is confined
in some high-rise hospital, her pelvis fractured
her front teeth scattered under the dash—coins
waiting to be tossed in a toll basket.

Each morning my teacher bent down
and whispered the same question . . .
Had my mother been released? (as if from prison).
Her red lipstick, the scent of coffee on her breath
made me sick—I felt at fault for each incorrect
not yet answer.

One Sunday morning my mother was deemed well
enough to venture to the hospital lobby to receive
my notes and stick-figure sketches. I wanted to hug
her but hung back—afraid of her witch-like smile
her halting gait behind a metal walker, her pretty face
sliced by a windshield's safety glass.

—Jenna Rindo

Poem and Prompt

Girlhood Landscape

My sister and I buy neon orange fingernail polish
and candy cigarettes. We steal strawberry
jam packets from the diner and sit by the railroad
tracks, painting our nails and sucking out jam. We are all
glossy. We jump from plank to plank with a stick
of candy between our fingers, smoking and skipping
over the boards like stones in a wide river. I tease
her hair up just like Reba McEntire. *You look so good,*
I say. The sky is a corset. It holds us
like breath. We put our last pennies on the rails
when we hear the train whistle miles down,
we jump back, stand just where the conductor can see us
hips out. *One day a boy will reach out of that train,* I say,
lift us up into the caboose like packages and think
of all the candy, the daylight, the lipgloss, the grape
pop, think of all that fun. But she doesn't want to,
her hand in mine, she says *what I want is to be here*
with you. On the way home,
I pick an orange tiger lily with my messy orange fingers,
because I want to remember blooming.
Because I think I could just bloom.

—Sara Moore Wagner

In this narrative poem, our first-person speaker captures a childhood memory, one filled with excitement and danger, feelings enhanced by the setting of the railroad tracks. The older of two sisters, the speaker has a desire to be grown up, so she buys nail polish and candy cigarettes. She thinks about boys. But the younger sister is enjoying her time of youthful innocence and just being with her big sister. To bring the scene alive, the poet uses present tense.

The poet uses a number of images, e.g., the neon orange nail polish and later the orange tiger lily picked by the older sister's *messy orange fingers*; the two sisters are *glossy*; they are *skipping over the boards like stones in a wide river*. And the wonderful image that closes the poem seems perfect: *I want to remember blooming. / Because I think I could just bloom.* How nicely this image emerges out of the picked orange tiger lily and the orange nail polish.

Notice the poet's interesting use of dialogue. Speaking in the first person, she inserts the words she spoke to her sister long ago and then the words her sister spoke to her. Thus we get three voices, and we get a contrast among those voices. The first-person speaker's present voice is mature while her earlier voice is on the threshold between childhood and adulthood and the younger sister's voice is one of youthful innocence.

✐ ✐ ✐

For your childhood memory poem, select an event that included one other person—a sibling, a different relative, or a friend.

Detail the setting. Make it a place that might, like the railroad tracks, represent a time of transition.

Use first-person narrator.

Use present tense.

Combine narrative with lyric elements. Include some metaphors and similes.

Include some images. Weave them throughout your poem.

Work in a color motif by focusing on a single color in your images.

Commentary: Coloring the Poem

—Sara Moore Wagner

I am someone who often uses color in poems, and it's in part because someone in a workshop once told me you shouldn't use color at all, and in part because I think a single color well-placed can be transportive visually. A shock of color, carefully juxtaposed, can burn an image into a reader's mind, as when Plath says, *Out of the ash / I rise with my red hair* in "Lady Lazarus." The juxtaposition of red hair and ash invokes the image of the phoenix and of fire and separates the speaker from the ash. It presents a full image in a few words.

"Girlhood Landscape" begins and ends in orange. I started with orange fingernail polish because I wanted to situate us in time and space, and I wanted to bring that stark juxtaposition to the poem. The girls in this poem are somewhere between children and teenagers, that space where the longing to become something bigger or more than what you are is intense. I attempt to show this with the nail polish, the jam lipgloss, the hair, the train. The girls are practicing at womanhood, or what they think that means. They are playing at adult in this poem. The orange is both tacky and childlike, and I hope it adds an impression that stays with the reader—one that's two-sided, a combination of yellow and red.

That orange polish feels very 90s, and like summer. Orange, which comes back at the end of the poem, is such an artificial and natural color—I'm thinking bright orange cheese powder and pollen. In the poem the girls have the orange fingers and the orange lily at the end to connect me, the speaker, who wanted so badly to be something else, to nature which is always becoming something else, despite itself. For me, orange is the one color to pull it all in—natural and artificial, tacky, a space between two things, the red burning of womanhood, and that yellow and golden summer of girlhood. I am hoping, then, that this whole poem is tinted orange, like that moment just before the day becomes something else.

Sample Poems

I Want to Be a Gladiola

but I'm chubby, thirteen, my braces just came off
and my mother plucked my eyebrows.
I've curled my hair and put on Tangee lipstick
and the bottle-green taffeta tulip-skirt dress
I made my mother buy me
for dinner with our relatives—Oh I am the epitome
of glamour, the *ne plus ultra* of seething flesh
in this cocktail dress for a 30-year-old,
and I goo-goo-eye the waiter, ready to elope with him
to the wilds of Colorado.
Meanwhile the aunt we've never met
asks my sister and me if we miss Japan,
how we like California, and our uncle, the rich lawyer,
grills our father, *So, what's next,*
now that you're finished with the Army?
1960, Beverly Hills, a place I hadn't heard of,
everybody coolly glittering.
As I chew my shrimp and sip my Shirley Temple,
the floor beneath the table suddenly gives way
to a pit called datelessness,
a breathless pit called you'll-never-find-love.
My *coupe glacée* arrives.
My Merry Widow's pinching,
and my garter belt makes welts on the backs of my thighs.

—Ann Fisher-Wirth

Skunk Cabbage

It is almost summer green, when my younger friend
from the third neighborhood hill, the one nearest the
woods, and I go in search of the skunk cabbage we
remember flourishing on a little island in the trickling
stream. We push through the underbrush, ferns tickling
our summer ankles, brambles scratching bare legs that
drop from our girlhood shorts. We're almost there, she
says, as I hold my finger to my lips to shush her, suddenly
hearing the rustle of something moving closer to our
kneeling bodies. *Maybe it's a deer*, I whisper, not yet
afraid. *Or maybe a stinky skunk*, she replies, smothering
a giggle. But then I hear voices, men voices, and the
careless tramp of heavy feet on broken branches.

Pulling her down with me, we drop to lie beside the stream,
still as the cabbage rooted in place, silent as the windless
trees whose limbs filter the sky's anonymous blue stare.
Let's go home now, I say, when the footsteps fade, fearing
what the men might have done to us. She doesn't want to
leave yet, feels safe when the voices fade into the foliage.
Let's dig up the skunk cabbage, she says, giggling, *and see
if it will grow in a garden*. But green as it is, I don't want to
touch it anymore, don't want to tear its roots from the suck
of marsh mud and drag its leaf-stench all the way home.

—Penny Harter

Poem and Prompt

Photo in a Photo

It's not the first time I've found
some ex-lover's profile on a dating
website, but this time it's *you*
in the shuffle, *your*
face in the lineup.
Behind you, in the photo
you've posted, are shelves
I assembled, counting out
the hardware and planks while
you read the *Times*,
a few feet away. I recognize
the spines of books I left
behind: Spanish I never learned,
guidebooks I marked with ink
and coffee. On one shelf,
light catches a silver frame—
you in the Andes, looking out
across a sunset-burnished
lake. I take a moment to relive
your steady gaze, my tender
focus—and it isn't that you put away
the photos of me from that trip,
it's that they were never there,
that interests me now; that
and the absence of sadness,
like a day in early spring,
that first step into morning light,
braced for cold that never comes.

—Lynn McGee

McGee uses a clever method to introduce her photo. The speaker
does not find the photo in an album but in a more contemporary

spot—a dating website. In the lineup of faces, she finds her ex-lover's face. But it's not her ex-lover's face that interests her; it's the background of the photo. There the first-person speaker sees the remnants of their former relationship: shelves she once assembled, books she left behind, and guidebooks *marked with ink / and coffee*.

The entire poem is a direct address as the speaker addresses someone who is living but not present. We quickly become aware of a single imagined auditor, a *you*, the ex-lover. And we have the delightful pleasure of listening in on what gives the impression of being a private conversation. This strategy results in a tone that's personal and private.

Notice how McGee uses details to characterize the ex-lover. The shelves the speaker built while the ex read the *Times* and the absence of any photos of the speaker suggest the ex-lover's coldness and lack of involvement.

Notice particularly what the poet does with light images: *light catches a silver frame—/ you in the Andes, looking out / across a sunset-burnished / lake*. Beautiful but also lonely—and missing the speaker. Then notice the stunning light image with which McGee closes the poem: her speaker feels *the absence of sadness, / like a day in early spring, / that first step into morning light, / braced for cold that never comes*. This lovely image expresses the speaker's lack of sorrow that the relationship ended. There is a tone of regret, but there's also a touch of irony here as the regret is not for what was lost but for what never was.

Before you begin your poem, first find or imagine a photo in a contemporary spot, e.g., Facebook, an alumni bulletin, a website, a newspaper, Instagram. Decide who's in the photo and what your relationship was or is. That person might be a lover but might instead be a parent, a teacher, a religious figure, a camp counselor.

In your draft, use a first-person speaker. Let the speaker talk directly to the subject in the photo. This technique of an imagined auditor is one you can use over and over. You will find that it releases you to say what you might not otherwise have said. You will also find that it gives the poem a strong voice. Try it.

As you proceed, describe the photo but limit the number of details so as to give each one heightened importance. Let the details in the photo characterize the auditor. Let them also reveal something about the speaker and the relationship. This is a very effective way of characterizing.

Finally, incorporate some images of light, darkness, and shadows. Use at least two.

Sample Poems

Leave Meeting

One of my professor friends posted a screenshot of his seminar,
the one he conducts for good students at a good school.
I see you there, center row, third from left.
My friend is in the little box next to you.
The famous guest author is the lower right corner.
Wish I could have been on that game show.

If you're here, it means you made it,
that you're not in permanent couch-surfing mode,
that you stopped drinking after those blackouts,
that you don't have a glove compartment rattling
with glass pipes and lighters,
that you kept a waitress job long enough to pay
a bit of rent and what it takes to join
this array of the bright and the bored.

So many of these students have the same white bookshelves
every influencer sits before these days.
Would they have the same books I read to you,
the ones you threw across the room
when the letters wouldn't stop dancing,
and that you had to read all over again the next year?
Would the sleeves of that hoody cover your tracks?

This is what I always hoped for you:
to know that not every brick building is a courthouse, or a jail;
not every group is a gang.
Even in this checkerboard you can almost read these lives—
the texts firing off off-line to the BFFs,
the renegotiations with OK, Boomer over
the unexpected homecoming.
You've been there, too.

If only you could have learned that not every grown man wants
something from you that takes the light out of your eyes,
the light I see in theirs, box by box,
the light I would see in your eyes
if only they would open in time.

—Bruce E. Whitacre
published in *North of Oxford*

After Seeing a Photograph of Flamingos (huddled together in the bathroom at Miami Zoo during Hurricane Andrew—August 24, 1992)

We are looking for safety
in the stalls where we share eyeliner and
wish our legs elegant stalks
like the pink birds now sheltering
on the black tiles grouted with years
of disappointment—one-sided crushes,
the urgency of urine, of toilet solace,
the feeling that each bathroom
is both utilitarian and shrink's office,
echoed calm broken by trickles and farts—
the close-up of failure and desire in the mirror,
each pore calling out for examination,
each eyelash freed of goop, wiped clean
while now the graceful arch of each bird beak
smiles and saddens for us. They are the same—
a flamboyance of flamingos the color of house insulation,
feathers and legs, cautious eyes waiting
out the hurricane the way we ducked
in the bathroom the nights of those dances,
elongated by hope, doused with other
people's judgment so that when we emerged
we were not relieved, only empty.

—Emily Franklin
published in *Channel Magazine*

Bonus Prompts: Imagery

—Adele Kenny

1. Take It to the Bank

To begin, create a a word bank including words pertaining to the current season. Next to each word, write an appropriate image. Now begin a poem with one of your images. As you continue to write, bring in words from your word bank and some additional images. Include some appropriate sensory details (sound, sight, taste, touch, smell). Use the images that are most striking and fresh.

2. To Sleep, Perchance to Create Images

Dreams, real or imagined, can provide rich inspiration for creating imagery. Begin by making a list of images that evoke the feeling of a dream you've had or one that you make up. That feeling might be eerie, peaceful, serene, disturbing, mystical. Next, select one of these images. Begin your poem with that image. As you write, add additional images. Try to show something about the dream and its impact. Make your dreamscape feel real.

3. The Real in Surreal

In poetry, Surrealism is characterized by images that are strange or unusual. A surreal image should contain an unusual juxtaposition. For example, a squirrel holding a cricket bat, a man with eyes on his hands, bubbles floating out of a tree. Now quickly make a list of surreal images. The idea is to be a little wild and to take risks with the images you create. Then begin your poem with one of your odd juxtapositions. Once you've begun writing, let your thoughts flow, even if they seem disjointed and unrelated. Your poem may or may not have an obvious meaning. That's okay. The imagery you create will allow subtle, unconscious meanings to enter your poem.

IV. Sound Devices

Be a songbird, not a parrot.

—Lawrence Ferlinghetti

Craft Talk: Reveling in Rhyme

—Annie Finch

What is it about rhyme that feels so deeply connected with the English language? Perhaps it's the easy way that it underscores the complex accentual-syllabic rhythms of English. Rhyme didn't arrive in English until the Middle Ages, from Arabic poetry by way of France and Spain. But today it is so interwoven with meter that when people say, *Poetry doesn't have to rhyme*, they usually mean they prefer free verse instead of meter, and when they say, *I like poetry that rhymes*, they often mean that they like poems in meter.

Like meter, rhyme revels in the deep playfulness of language. Physiologically, it activates the right brain—the unconscious—and threatens the dominance of our logical left brains. I believe that's why poets have been suspicious of it, why Thomas Campion attacked it as *childish* and Milton called it the *invention of a barbarous age*. Many of us still associate unrhymed poetry with authority and sincerity, and rhyme with silly, childish self-indulgence. After all, if you're willing to change what you're saying to make it rhyme, how seriously could you have meant it in the first place?

Very seriously, in my experience! The often-surprising contributions of rhyme can make a poem feel more authentically true, more deeply grounded in the mysteries of life. I see meaning as multifaceted and holistic rather than linear, so I like rhyme, when it's done well, for exactly the reasons that Milton disliked it, even when done well: rhyme poses a threat to the ego's control by inviting in the unexpected—and the physical.

I've encountered some of my greatest poetic challenges—and satisfactions—when writing in heavily rhymed forms. The most intense was the Celtic form known as Awdl Gwyddyd, which I used for "Brigid," addressed to the Celtic Goddess of Poetry. This form requires combinations of interlocking rhymes, including between the line ending and the middle of the line: *Hammers **fall** / the gold will **all** be beaten.* Such poems are exciting to write and can be fascinating to read. The rhymes act almost like stitches that tie the poem down, suggesting with a thrill of danger that otherwise it could have the power to float us away, out of ourselves.

Here is some advice on rhyming that I share with poets I teach.

1. Don't be embarrassed to use a rhyming dictionary. I learned this healthy attitude from my dear friend Agha Shahid Ali, who learned it from James Merrill. Shahid told me that Merrill had worn out several rhyming dictionaries in his life.

2. *Exact* or *perfect* rhymes are defined as rhymes where the stressed vowels of two words, and any sounds that follow, are the same: *finger, linger*. But rhymes don't have to be exact to be moving and exciting. In *slant* rhymes (sometimes called *half rhymes* or *near rhymes*), either the vowels or the consonants are similar but not the same. For inspiring examples of slant rhymes, read Emily Dickinson, who rhymed *soul* with *all*, *death* with *earth*, and *away* with *eternity*. The *Oxford Rhyming Dictionary* includes slant rhymes.

3. Obvious and intense rhymes don't need to be avoided. Gwendolyn Brooks, for example, uses audacious, conspicuous rhymes with great skill: *knee* and *satinly*, *thinking* and *stinking*, *twinges* and *fringes*. As long as the rest of the poem is strong enough to stand up to the rhymes, and as long as they add to the meaning of the poem, go for it.

4. Rhyme not with words, but with phrases. This comes from Robert Frost, who practiced what he preached with rhymes like these: *leaves got up in a coil and hissed, / Blindly struck at my knee and missed.*

Today rhyme is stronger than ever, with *rhyming* being used as a synonym for *rapping*, rhyming apps and dictionaries proliferating along with contests and recordings, and a mega performer named *Busta Rhymes*. Rhyme doesn't need to hamper poets. Instead it can, as Samuel Daniel put it in 1603, give us wings—to travel *beyond our power to a farre happier flight.*

Poem and Prompt

Diagnosis in Reverse

First, the witch turning from the door
made of spiced cake

and sugared almonds. Then the birds
offering the bread back

to the forest floor, the children
skipping backwards into the gaunt

yawn of the house as the mother's
long hunger begins

to soften, her hearth dark with smoke.
And then a spark,

the children in the back orchard
eating apricots heavy

with juice. Pale cream in a bowl. A vase
of primroses. Foxglove stirring

outside the open window. The father
coming up the summer path, easy

with evening. Hansel humming.
Fresh bread and long light, long light.

    —Kate Gaskin

The poet begins with a title that seems to have little to do with
the poem that follows. There is no diagnosis in the poem;
instead, we find the fairy tale of Hansel and Gretel told in

reverse. This apparent lack of connection raises the possibility that the poem is a metaphor. The title, then, is a clue to the significance of the poem. Haven't we all had a moment when something terrible happened that made us wish for a return to yesterday? Certainly, a bad diagnosis would ignite such a wish. Perhaps the real story is too hard to tell. The screen of the fairy tale provides safety. This screen also adds a layer of subtlety and sophistication to the poem.

The poem begins towards the end of the fairy tale with the witch at the door, but here she turns away. The children do not enter. The crumbs left by Hansel and Gretel as a trail to lead them back home are now returned to the forest by the birds that had eaten them. The speaker moves us back to the children's mother when she was still happy, before her *long hunger begins*. By the end of the poem, the children are home again, as if they'd never left. All is well.

Notice the sensuous images Gaskin uses: the *hearth dark with smoke. / And then a spark, the children eating apricots heavy // with juice. Pale cream in a bowl. A vase / of primroses inside.* And then the closing image: *Fresh bread and long light, long light.*

Notice the subtle use of sound devices and repetition, e.g., the rhyme of *dark* and *spark* and the near rhyme of *gaunt* and *yawn*; the *k* consonance of *dark, smoke, spark*, and *back*; the *e* assonance of *easy* and *evening*. Notice the alliteration of *bread back; forest floor, foxglove, father*, and *Fresh*; and *Hansel humming*. Finally, notice the repetition in the last image, its two alliterative *l* words repeated: *long light, long light*.

For your bad news poem, choose a bad experience or a time when you received terrible news that made you wish you could reverse Time, when you wished you could unravel the experience back to yesterday. Think about the steps or days leading up to the bad moment. Now think about those steps in reverse.

Locate another story that might serve as a screen or a metaphor for your story. This should be a story that begins in a good place but ends in a bad one. Perhaps a fairy tale, a biblical story, something from mythology. Make a chronological list of the details of that story.

In your draft tell that second story in reverse chronological order. In other words, begin at the end of your list. Make references to the specific details of the story.

Pepper the retelling with images drawn from the story.

Improve the language and music of your poem with some sound devices and repetition. End with the repetition of a significant phrase. Try to word that phrase alliteratively. Does that work to the poem's advantage? If not, feel free to delete it.

Give your poem a title that suggests the poem's real subject, one that serves as a lens through which the poem may be read.

Sample Poems

Undoing Third-Degree Burns

Like a polaroid,
    Eurydice appeared

from the darkness
    and inched backwards

into the underworld. This time,
    Orpheus didn't turn his head

at the echo of her footsteps.
    Instead, he took out his lyre

and sang his lament in a slow,
    mournful reverse.

Step by step, they walked past
    Persephone and Hades

and Cerberus until they were
    above ground and up to their knees

in the sweetest grasses.
    All around them, peonies

and sunflowers outstretched their petals
    like hands greeting them.

The viper that had bitten
    Eurydice slunk back as

the triangle-shaped
    wound on her leg eased.

Newly wed, Eurydice and Orpheus
    sat under a tree.

They posed as if in front of a camera,
    waiting for the photo

to capture the time when
    they thought they'd have forever.

The sunlight licked their skin,
    again, again.

      —Shannon K. Winston

Unstepping into Divorce

after Kate Gaskins' "Diagnosis in Reverse"

The grey wolf howls beside the house,
transfixed on a slip of cotton tail silvered

in cottage light. Inside, the grandmother
drinks cups of mint tea, drifts back into sleep

until lungs clear their ballooned exhale.
Flowers go unpicked by little hands,

daffodils and lilacs left to a wood's open
chest. Always, the path leads home to

the village, girl beside the oven
watching dough transform into bread.

Her mother churns butter to keep
for themselves. Collection of berry cakes

cool on handmade towels, apple shapes
unstitched into blood red spools.

Sheep in the fields are unshorn,
their untouched wool like pearls against

the trees. See: the madder root nestled
underground, sleeping warm, sleeping warm.

—Christen Noel Kauffman

Poem and Prompt

Nashville After Hours

Late night in a honky-tonk, fried pickles
in a red plastic basket, and it was all Loretta
on the heel-bruised stage, sung by a big girl
we kind of both had a crush on. Nashville
got the best of us, in a bar shootin' Fireball
with the band that just roused the Ryman.
Good grief we were loaded, shotguns,
and the soft-hearted. It's like this:
sometimes the buried buzz comes back,
and soon the kid that cut the lunch line
ain't nothing; and the cruel tongues licking
your insides are gone; the bully girl who
kicked you out of the city is no one, no rotten
crumb left, just a dizzy river of nonsense
in the waxy light under the bright signs and
look here, I won't deny it: I was there,
standing in the bar's bathroom mirror,
saying my name like I was somebody.

       —Ada Limón

Notice that the title provides both a place and a time—information the poet now does not have to include in the poem. Limón then begins with some local color and some sensory details. We hear honky-tonk music, taste fried pickles and the cinnamon-flavored Fireball, see the color red and the damaged stage of the Ryman auditorium (formerly the home of the Grand Ole Opry).

The poem turns at the end of line 8 with *It's like this:* and then we get to the substance of the poem, the reason why the speaker loves this music—it allows her to shed bad memories.

The colon is followed by a list of memories of experiences that leave us bruised.

Line 8 also signals an interesting shift in point of view from first-person plural *We* to second-person *you*. That's a risk, but it works; it brings us into the poem and makes us feel spoken to and understood. Another shift is signaled by *look here*. The speaker now uses first-person singular, and the poem becomes personal.

Notice the speaker's down-to-earth diction. She uses the colloquial expressions *look here* and *Good grief*. She uses the bad grammar of *ain't* and adds to that a double negative with *nothing*.

This poem appears simple but is loaded with craft. Let's consider the various devices of sound. We have straight internal rhyme in *light* and *bright*, near rhyme in *night* and *fried* and in *plastic basket*. We have an abundance of alliteration: *best, bar, band, buried buzz, back* and *lunch line, licking*. We have assonance: *buzz, cut, lunch, tongues* and *kicked* and *dizzy river*. And consonance in *crush* and *Nashville*. Such a trove of sound devices makes this poem a pleasure to read aloud.

The predominance of ten- to twelve-syllable lines, the monosyllabic words, and the stressed syllables give the poem a perceivable rhythm. Read it aloud and you'll hear and feel the rhythm.

✐ ✐ ✐

Let's do a poem that relies on sensory details. First choose a place and a time—be specific, e.g., Cape Cod in October, New York City before sunrise, Paterson at dinnertime. Use your place and time as your title.

Brainstorm a list of sensory details that pertain to your subject. Cover a variety of senses—give us something to taste, something to hear, to smell, to feel, to see. Then begin your draft with those details. Get in some specifics; fried pickles is better than snacks, Fireball is better than whiskey.

About eight lines in, turn the poem with something like *It's like this* or *Here's how it happens* or *This is what's known* or *These are facts, for sure.* At this point bring in a shift in point of view. This is the central challenge of this poem, so don't skip it. Let this part of the poem be a list of some kind. Let the list build up intensity. Shift the point of view a second time towards the end of the poem. If you follow the model, you'll begin with first-person plural, shift to second person, shift to first-person singular. It might work, it might not work; you're not married to it.

As you move to subsequent drafts, work in a few colloquialisms, e.g., *for Pete's sake, holy cow, gosh darn.* How about a bit of bad grammar?

Pay attention to devices of sound. Work with monosyllables, get in some internal rhymes, some near rhymes, alliteration, assonance, and consonance. Pay attention to your language; let it make music.

Sample Poems

Latonia Racetrack at Cooldown

We sat on the tack trunk munching
fried egg sandwiches, watching the parade
of horses bundled in their heavy blankets
take their slow constitutionals between the barns.
Now and then there was a pause for water,
the pail rattling against the lead chain.
There were melodic neigh echoes,
that gritty clop an iron shoe makes
on scattered gravel. Then the lights clunked off
at the grandstand, the world fading to slumber
as hands and horses ambled between
the manure piles. Here's the thing:
you realize the atmosphere is the same
for both winning and losing horses,
the same calm settles over their shoulders
like those thick blankets. This isn't the time
for recriminations or penalties. You think,
this is how it is and should be after a race,
regardless of ambitions and wagers.
Shoot, I've both won and lost many a contest
and never known that kind of tranquility,
that sense of reward earned for an honest effort,
either in defeat or victory. I like their way better.
Come down easy, sleep deep and well.
Tomorrow we'll start thinking about that next race.

—Nancy Susanna Breen

Desperado, Slightly Drunk and Off-Key

after Ada Limón

The fancy reunion dinner out on the lawn
has wound down, even the after-parties
have broken up, but we have peanuts and beer
and a few guitars and a little talent
and we all have flights in the morning
but nobody wants to say goodnight
so we pass the beer and somebody
opens a bottle of red and somebody
sings "Desperado." And listen, sometimes
your voice cracks on the high notes
and sometimes you come in a beat too soon
but feel that scratch in your throat,
feel that strain of unused muscle?
How it all comes back—
how you used to sing in the car
late at night, coming home from the club
or the party where you danced like you knew
every eye was on you, where you got up close
and sweaty and soft and you weren't afraid yet
of what hands could do to your body,
of how a mouth on your mouth could silence you,
back when you could still take a man by the hand
and walk off into the shadows believing
in his promise of sweetness. And how long
has it been since you rolled down the windows
and turned up the volume, how long
since you sent that cry out into the night?
I won't deny it: I can't sing worth a damn
but here I am not giving a damn
because I better unlock my throat
and get this song out
before it's too late.

—Jennifer Saunders
published in *San Pedro River Review*

Poem and Prompt

My Mother's Heart in Troubling Times

Her heart of brass, her heart of tin,
skin-thin heart of gold, heart of sin,

heart of glass, of flesh and flask,
her chicken-liver wussy-dither heart of hearts,

she eats it out, starts at the base, her yellow heart,
her purple heart, her crossed-and-hope-to-lie heart,

hard heart, soft and heavy heart,
light and lively heart, she eats it

bare and aching, broken, beating,
her stopped heart berating her heart-stood-still,

her standing-stone of a heart,
heart pinned to her sleeve,

heart pining for sleep,
her faint-hearted, hope-to-fly heart,

her never-catch-a-man heart,
heart in her mouth, heart in her boot,

oh her sinking heart,
skipping-a-beat heart,

the heart of those heart-to-heart-talks heart,
its cockles, its chambers, its snail

of a heart creeping along now, the heart
she never had, the heart she never had

in it, she eats it, she eats her heart out—
lets her heart do her heart some good.

—Lois Marie Harrod

The speaker identifies her mother's heart as the subject of the poem, and she focuses on that throughout the poem. The word *heart* appears in all but one line and in most lines it appears more than once. This use of repetition drives the poem relentlessly forward. We never do find out what the *troubling times* of the title refers to, but we know that the heart responds by devouring itself, an image the poet repeats four times.

Other devices of sound also drive the poem. We have end rhyme in the first stanza's *tin* and *sin*. We have internal rhyme between the *brass* of stanza 1 and the *glass* of stanza 2. Alliteration is abundant: *flesh and flask* in stanza 2, *hard heart* and *heavy heart* in stanza 4. We also have assonance with *aching* and *berating* in stanza 4 and consonance with *heart in her boot* in stanza 8.

It seems as if the poet compiled a list of heart-related expressions and then employed them in a list poem: *hard heart, heart-stood-still, heart pinned to her sleeve, sinking heart, standing stone of a heart, yellow heart, purple heart,* and so on. Into this list she also tosses the quirky colloquialism of *chicken-liver wussy-dither heart of hearts* as well as two rhyming alterations of the "cross my heart and hope to die" expression: *hope-to-lie heart* and *hope-to-fly heart.*

The poet does something interesting with point of view: the title includes the first-person *My*, but the poem itself never uses a first-person pronoun—no *I*, no *my*—so the poem appears to be third person—note the use of *she* and *her*—but we are always aware of the first-person speaker's presence.

All of these elements get mixed together in a one-sentence poem. The poem has no full stops until the very end, until the heart stops beating. Only then does the single sentence stop.

Because the poem observes other elements of grammar and moves relentlessly forward, the reader very likely does not notice that the poem is one sentence. But that structure adds forward momentum to the poem.

✍ ✍ ✍

Let's do a body part poem. First, get a person in mind, e.g., a family member, a lover, an enemy, a neighbor. Then select one body part as the focus of your poem, perhaps the liver, brain, stomach, eye, or tongue. Now compile a list of expressions related to the body part. Feel free to alter some of the expressions. Add several quirky phrases to your list.

Use your list to quickly compose a first draft. If you write fast, you'll be more likely to get the fast pace you want for this poem.

As you work on subsequent drafts, make use of the same devices of sound that Harrod employs: rhyme, alliteration, assonance, consonance. Especially capitalize on repetition.

Take on the challenge of making this a single-sentence poem.

Give your poem a title that identifies your person, body part, and situation. Challenge yourself to do with point of view what Harrod has done—first-person pronoun in the title, third-person pronouns throughout the poem.

Commentary: My Mother's One-Sentence Heart

—Lois Marie Harrod

In "Fast Break," certainly one of the great one-sentence poems, Edward Hirsch uses a single action—his friend Dennis Turner's relentless rush to the hoop—as a metaphor for Turner's life, a dash that in its end becomes an *orange blur / floating perfectly through the net.*

Instead of a single action, I use a continuous action, the beating heart. "My Mother's Heart in Troubling Times" is a one-sentence *list poem* (one that uses just about every conceivable cliché about the heart) in order to power the poem to its blessing, my mother letting *her heart do her heart some good.* I don't specify my mother's troubling times; rather I use the trite, sometimes varied and punned upon, to say something new about endurance and compassion.

In fact, the poem began one morning when I came across a long list of clichés that use the word *heart.* The repetition of the word *heart* becomes the engine that keeps the poem beating just as my mother kept her heart, hard and heavy, light and lively, going through her troubling times—until the sentence, until her sentence was finished.

Sample Poems

My Mother's Hands

her bark hands, her scaled hands,
her useless red and blotchy hands,

her can't open a can hands, can't slap
the cat hands,

butcher hands, gizzard hands,
brained the rabbit quick hands,

hands that pruned the apple trees,
mucked and limed the stall,

hands that gripped
the dervish whip,

threw away the dog,
God hands, saw hands,

five acres of fence hands,
twist hands, fist hands,

made me ride a bronco hands,
bone hands, ash hands,

blood under the skin hand,
hands that wrapped me,

washed me, dried me,
buttoned me, braided me,

hands that did whatever
they wanted to me,

for as long as they could.

—Dion O'Reilly

He'd Promised All of Us His Hand

When she still thought he loved her, she told us,
the apartment was handy to have at hand,
her hand warm on the brass doorknob,

and he'd have his hands full, their love
wild, and after he left, she'd lie on the bed
and make animal shadows on the wall

with her hands in the stream of the streetlight—
her empty hands, soft hands—and she
only sort of minded that he never lent a hand

with cleaning up—she his handmaiden—
she had to hand it to him, really,
and besides, she felt herself in good hands,

hands down the best hands, strong, handsome
hands, and never a single spot of dirt
under a fingernail, dark hands to hold

her, and when he waved goodbye,
by some sleight of hand, his hand
became her heart, fluttering, so when

she learned he'd had no hand in selecting
the gifts he'd handed her—familiar to us—
the silver box there on the dresser,

the hand-blown striped blue pitcher,
the leather handbag hanging from the chair—
when she confirmed he'd handed off

his shopping to his assistant, who'd bought
ten of each selection—two hands' worth!—
on the one hand, she wanted to wash

her hands of the apartment, but on the other,
it was her one bird in the hand,
and it was time—past time—to take matters

into her own hands, her handwriting
lovely on the small invitations
which she had the assistant deliver by hand

to each of us nine other women—
a party of revelation to be held at the apartment
where the gifts were prominently to hand—

the pitcher in the entryway filled with flowers,
red roses like he used to hand each of us
(these too the handiwork of his assistant).

—Lisken Van Pelt Dus

Bonus Prompts: Sound Devices

—Michael T. Young

1. Sorrow and Apocopated Rhyme

Rhyme is perhaps the most obvious sonic device in a poet's toolbox, especially end rhyme. But a poet can create more subtle echoing effects by embedding the rhymes inside other words, as in apocopated rhymes. Apocopated rhyme is when the stressed syllable of a two-syllable word is rhymed with a single, stressed syllable as in *wedding/bed* or *fancy/pants*. Write a poem about a time when you cried for someone else's sorrow. This could be for someone in real life or for a character in a movie or book. Employ apocopated rhymes. See if you can place the words near enough to each other to hear them echo, but not loud enough to be too immediately obvious.

2. Lost in Alliteration

Write a poem about something you lost and never found. Employ alliteration at least three times. Play with how far apart you place the alliterated words: sometimes fitting them into a single line and sometimes spreading them out over two lines. See which effect works best for your poem. Too close, and the alliterated words might clang. Too far apart, and they might lose their connection.

3. Being Formal with Consonance

Set yourself the goal of writing a formal poem about your favorite or least favorite food item. The poem can be in strict meter, accentual lines, or syllabic lines, whichever you choose. Rather than a fixed form like a sonnet, use something like quatrains rhyming *abab, cdcd,* and so on. But instead of using exact rhymes, use consonance. Repeat consonant sounds, for example, *wade/guide, defend/mind, teeter/cat.* This can be a powerful device for creating internal echoes throughout a poem.

V. Repetition

When you have exhausted all possibilities,
remember this—you haven't.

—Thomas Edison

Craft Talk: Playing It by Ear

—David Graham

Of all the tools in the kit, repetition may be the most versatile as well as most primal. Versatile because it is no single technique but a myriad; a poet can repeat just about anything, whether a certain sound, stanzaic pattern, or phrase, and possibly create something shapely. I call repetition primal because it is the bedrock of poetic form—all form, really. From the crib we love a beat, sonic or visual recurrence, symmetry, and so forth. Which is why most religious and civic as well as familial rituals contain a good deal of repetition. Long before there were books or even written language, we had chant, incantation, litany.

Of course, repetition is necessary but not sufficient, and must be in continual tension with its opposite. To avoid monotony and predictability, the poem needs at least some shifts in idea or music. As Ezra Pound phrased it, "Verse consists of a constant and a variant." The more some repetitive element is foregrounded, the sharper the contrast will need to be.

Consider, for example, Barbara Ras's "You Can't Have It All," a brilliant list poem. List poems are repetitive by nature, with repeated phrasing or syntax, and each item listed pertaining to the same idea. Note the lengthy series of parallel clauses with anaphora, as Ras lists items that *you can have* though *you can't have it all*. A passage from the middle of the poem gives a sense of the poem's moves:

> You can visit the marker on the grave
> where your father wept openly. You can't bring back the dead,
> but you can have the words *forgive* and *forget* hold hands
> as if they meant to spend a lifetime together. And you can
>   be grateful
> for makeup, the way it kisses your face, half spice, half
>   amnesia . . .

Ras threads her necessary contrasts throughout. The poem's structure is essentially circular, ending where it began, like a song.

I'm a firm fan of writing prompts of all sorts: whatever launches you and leads somewhere productive is to be welcomed. When I taught workshops, I assigned many and various exercises. I noticed that often the simplest ones, involving basic repetitions, were most effective for many students. That seemed normal; they could move on to more complicated ones as their writing matured and their skills sharpened.

But over time a funny thing happened: my own presumably more sophisticated writing methods gravitated back toward simplicity. I've come to know I work best by improvisation on simple triggers, which for me frequently involve those basics of primal repetition—anaphora and the list. They provide me with a basic rhythmic grounding and ensure some momentum from the start.

My initial drafts often consist of what I call *riffing:* lifting an idea, image, phrase, or metaphor from a poem or other source and then, without much forethought, playing the changes on it. The results can be messy and forgettable, but often they produce associative leaps and out-of-nowhere phrases that only my subconscious mind could serve up. Rapid-fire anaphora is often where many of my poems begin, though not necessarily where they end.

I'll conclude with one example from my own practice. A few years ago I was savoring Robert Bly's loose adaptations of the ghazal form in some of his later books. His repeated lines and phrases are clearly very improvisatory. Inspired equally loosely by his example, one day I took a line I love from "The Sympathies of the Long-Married" as my prompt. *Most of the time, we live through the night,* Bly concluded one stanza. I began riffing on that idea, taking his line as my first line, then reaching for my old friend anaphora for the second line. *Most of the time the dark waters rise / then fall into sun and birdsong,* I wrote, without the faintest idea where I was headed.

Whenever I got stuck, I just scribbled *most of the time* again, and followed where my mind wandered, jumping in Bly-like fashion from image to image. Near the end I found myself quoting a line from Virgil and recounting a childhood memory, and I still have no notion where all that came from, though Bly gets partial credit, I suppose, for his inspirational leaping.

At the revision stage I had to do some shifting and tinkering, but in this rare case the general shape of the draft looked solid from the start. I knew I had a keeper. After some rewrites I wound up with five quatrains and seven iterations of *most of the time*, including using it as the title. It appears twice in the first stanza, to set the pulse; then once in each of the remaining stanzas, always at a different spot in the quatrain. Twice it's tucked into dependent clauses, and once the phrase is broken across two lines. These syntactical variations were by ear; I've been writing long enough to know that as soon as you start repeating, you need to vary the rhythm. At this point, both repetition and variation felt primal.

Poem and Prompt

Facetime

My wife and I sit out on the sun deck
with our coffee every morning.
Do you want to grill tonight,
she asks, or should I make something?
And if she cooked something last night
I'll say, you cooked something last night
so why don't I grill? And if I grilled last night
I'll say, I grilled last night, so
why don't you cook something?
And this conversation makes sense
and is reassuring. Meanwhile

a coyote trotted down our boring
little suburban street yesterday,
right here in Cleveland Heights
like he owned the place. And I read
that monkeys are ransacking shops
in India, and jackals are wandering
the streets of Tel Aviv, and water
buffalo are just kind of standing around
on the empty highways of New Delhi,

while in the closed down Tokyo Aquarium
these tiny eels—garden eels, they're called—
are forgetting what we look like.
The zookeepers are worried
that the eels are getting lonely,
so they've hung iPads on the tanks.
They ask on their website, "Could you please
show your face to the eels from your home?"

And of course everyone is phoning the eels
which makes sense and is reassuring.

The skies are so blue it startles
the starlings into arabesques.
The seas are so quiet that the whales,
for once, can hear themselves think.
As I stand in my driveway grilling tonight
I feel grateful to the eels. How nice
of them to miss us, after all we've done.
Such magnanimity in a beast so small.
I decide to give them a call.

—George Bilgere

Bilgere has given his poem a title that has various meanings. The word *Facetime* might refer to the program on a Mac computer that allows face-to-face chats. It might also refer to time spent in person with someone else. It might refer to seeing someone's face. This is an effective title because it suggests several ideas to our heads.

The poet focuses on a time of isolation from the outside world but togetherness with one other person. The first-person speaker begins with the sort of trivial conversation that couples often engage in. Notice that the first stanza includes three questions. The questions, while trivial, are made more interesting as the poet uses word order reversals: *Do you want to grill tonight, / she asks, or should I make something? / And if she cooked something last night / I'll say, you cooked something last night, / so why don't I grill?*

Notice also that the first stanza is filled with repetitions, e.g., the words *something, cook, cooked,* and *last night.* The speaker concludes this stanza with *And this conversation makes sense / and is reassuring.* This statement is reiterated in the second to last stanza. The questions and the repetitions create a casual tone, and because the conversation is between two people, there's also a tone of intimacy.

In stanza 2 the speaker offers a list of what's going on in the world beyond where he is. This list emphasizes the isolation and loneliness and, perhaps, the coziness of his own small world. The list ends with an image of eels who've grown lonely during the absence of sightseers to their zoo. This wonderful image returns at the end of the poem

Finally, notice the strategic bit of rhyme that ends the poem. Although Bilgere has not used rhyme throughout the poem, his last two lines employ a masculine rhyme, i.e., one between stressed syllables. His rhyming words are not big, important words but two little ones: *small* and *call*. This simple technique grabs our attention and makes a strong ending.

✐ ✐ ✐

For your own poem of isolation, recall a period of extended separation from others. It might be the pandemic of 2020-21, but it might also be a period of extended illness or recuperation after surgery, a time when you moved to a new location, or a time when you switched to a new school or job. Jot down some recollections of your isolation.

Begin your draft using a first-person speaker. Include no more than one other person. Or you might include no one. Raise some questions.

Pepper the poem liberally with repetitions. Overdo it in this first draft. Try your hand at the word order reversal strategy.

Include a list of what you were missing during this time—not simply the things you longed for but what was happening that you weren't part of. Consider the world beyond where you were. Be sure that your list includes a few strong images.

End your draft with a repetition of a single image from your list. Make it work for the poem.

Try Bilgere's simple rhyme strategy in your last two lines.

Give your poem a title with multiple meanings.

As you revise, you may want to cut back on the repetitions and the items in your list.

Sample Poems

One Thing I Desire

Like leaves shredded from a winter-stormed tree,
somewhere else teases, just beyond what I can see.
Branches tangle with vines, clack in icy cocoons,
but a bit of blue beckons.
                                        Too much time alone
finds me addicted to self, even if, like Frodo of the Shire,
I began this journey in good faith, a service to others.

Now the novelty, the adventure of all I can do
from one house, one room has flattened my horizon
and forged a ring of *one* around all I do, all I say
to the virtual world.
                                        I am a collection of atoms colliding,
hurling bits and bytes of electrons across the atmosphere
to Kansas, Florida, Ireland
to gather in separate spaces on one screen—
time meaningless.
                                        Sun and moon nudged ever farther
until fog and ice demand our witness.
Lights out. Networks down.
                                        We wander the darkness.
Each clover leaf just fragile enough to tear
but rooted together gentling the fall.

I want to see, to know you. I want to touch you again.

—KB Ballentine

Expirations

All your private prescriptions to me, the new
nurse, the adrenalin rush that came from our
mutual crush are long past effective date with
no remaining refills. The notes you left for me
hidden in the cabinet above the locked narcotics
drawer—I have burned to ashes. Once I waited
until the end of my twelve-hour shift then read
them after I clocked out and was riding the morning
Metro home, feet swollen under opaque white
support hose, part of the unit dress code. Each
scribbled phrase I read like a pain pill to be taken
only as needed. You parceled a lock of your ginger
hair into a package of cotton gauze—perhaps for me
to use for some version of voodoo to claim you.

We spiked with fever, you and I, then soured, old
cream that curdled, ruined the strong coffee I
relied on for quiet shifts. Our clandestine connection
suffered vague symptoms. A blood sample sent to the lab
for culture came back negative for specific pathogens.

I quit that special care unit, moved deeper
south, way beyond the Mason Dixon line,
started over, burned all your letters, the scrawled
words—illegible—the worn paper contaminated.
I took a job at a hospital lost in some pre-bellum
time. I measured vital signs and charted surgical
incisions—on the longest graveyard shifts, complicated
with failed resuscitations, I rode the elevator down,
closed my eyes until the doors chimed open, too
tired to take the stairs, reached into my pocket
for a folded note that wasn't there.

—Jenna Rindo

Poem and Prompt

"still in a state of uncreation"

Little eradicator. Little leaser.
Little loam collector, connoisseur
of each vestigial part. Little bundle
of nerve. Waste leaker. Pump.
Little lead-in, lean-to, least known,
lucky landing. Bean, being, borne
by me. Little consequence.
Little ruckus causer. Unborn.
Little insatiable. Little irrevocable.
Little given. Little feared.
Little living. Little seen. Little
dangler. Little delight. Little
growing. Little life. Little you.

                    —Camille Dungy

The title of this poem grabs our attention because it's in quotation marks. According to a note at the end of Dungy's book, *Trophic Cascade*, the title is a phrase borrowed from a sentence in the "Anger and Tenderness" chapter of Adrienne Rich's *Of Woman Born: Motherhood as Experience and Institution*. The title becomes one of many descriptive phrases in this poem of direct address. The descriptive phrases are about the speaker's unborn child. Notice, however, that it's only at the end of the poem that the speaker makes a direct address to her subject: *Little you.*

Looking closely, we realize that there are no sentences in the poem, only fragments. And only one (nearly hidden) verb! Nevertheless, Dungy lobs out the phrases so quickly that even without verbs the pace builds up throughout the poem and makes us feel the speaker's anticipation, her eagerness to meet her baby.

Dungy also grabs our attention with the repetition of the word *little* which appears eighteen times in this short poem. We notice too the alliteration of *l* words, e.g., *Little leaser, Little loam, Little lead-in, lean-to,* and *least known.*

Adding to the music created by repetition and alliteration is assonance—notice the soft *i* sound repeated in *Little living* and the long *i* sound in *delight* and *life*; notice the soft *u* sound in *bundle, Unborn, ruckus*; and notice the long *e* sound in *bean, being,* and *me.* Finally, notice the repetition of the *er* and *or* sounds at word endings: *eradicator, leaser, collector, connoisseur, leaker, causer, dangler.*

For your own poem of repetition, first find an intriguing line or phrase in a piece of prose, one you could use as the springboard into your own poem. It should make you think of someone or something that is unable or unlikely to reply. Use this phrase in quotation marks as the title of your poem.

With your subject/auditor in mind, brainstorm a list of descriptive phrases of varying lengths.

Cobble these phrases together in your first draft. Speak directly to your auditor, but bring in a *you* only towards the end of the draft. The poem will gain intimacy from this move.

No complete sentences. If verbs sneak in, get them out. Allow no more than one verb. Tackle this linguistic challenge.

Revise the poem with your ear tuned for music. Be sure to focus on repetition; find a key word in your draft and repeat it throughout the poem. Also work in some alliteration. Capitalize on assonance. The repetition of sound devices will add music to your poem.

Commentary: Repeating Myself

—Camille Dungy

Consistency breeds apathy. The beauty of repetition lies in the occasional disruption of repetition: Expectation and reward. Expectation and reward. Expectation, expectation. Surprise! A writer might build a little nest in a poem, a comfortable place for the reader's mind to rest (the material for this nest might be rhyme, might be repetition of words or phrases, might be consistency of images or ideas), but even as she makes this space of comfort, she must be aware that too much comfort breeds disinterest.

Expectation and reward. Expectation and reward. Expectation, expectation. Are you listening? You are listening? Really? Well then, here's what you've expected: your reward. That's a forced attenuation strategy that doesn't even call significantly on the content of the words. Even if you weren't listening to the words, you could hear the music of them—like the songs we sing our children, the lyrics of which are often quite dark and distressing, though the melodies sound nice. This is a way to raise the threat of danger in the midst of calm. It is also a way to create calm in the midst of danger. Create a pattern, reward that pattern, and disrupt that pattern—but rather than leaving the poem in that state of disruption, return to the pattern.

Around the time I wrote "still in a state of uncreation," I was thinking deeply about what it means to formulate a pattern of repetition and then to disrupt that pattern. How long can a poem retain its tension, and the reader's attention, before you have to turn the poem in an unexpected direction? I was having fun implementing various strategies for repetition in this poem. Words like *little* and sounds like the *l* or *b* or *ean* sounds get repeated to near exhaustion, but hopefully not beyond the point of exhaustion. And then something new happens, which may or may not be a new source of something to repeat. It was fun to play in this way, but the work was part of something I was seriously interested in as well.

Sample Poems

"as leaky a vessel as was ever made"

The Faraway Nearby
—Rebecca Solnit

Full of stories, full of holes.
A hole in the whole thing.
Full of yourself. Full of it.

A habit of holding forth.
A string of stories, gussied up to glorify.
Pie in the sky. Tall tales, sound and fury.
Perforated. Punctured junctures.
A sieve-sifter, shape-shifter,
a grifter full of gab. A power grab,
a sugar-coated hero's tale,
a magnifying glass, inflating.

A yacht? (Not). More a dinghy,
glitter-glossed and underwater.
Short story long, not wrong,
but over-blown and over-rated.
Flash memoir fleshy as novel—
pompous, porous, pervious.
Cheeky ego, leaky cuss.

—Jayne Brown

"the whole earth is like a poem"

"The Sun"
—Czeslaw Milosz

the fulsome moon, the dancing bay, circling
glitter-light. Sculpted mountains, clouds above
the glassy sea, the cinnabar sunset. The call
of the shofar, an ostentation of peacocks, cedar tree
sproutings from bird droppings. Sparks of fireflies,
scattered stars. Wildflower. Apple blossom. Azalea
ablaze. Dramatic forsythia. Bluebell constancy.
Birdweed, Birch, Bird's foot. Courage of poplars,
humility of cherry trees. Indeed lilac. Indeed jasmine.
Delight, delighted, endeared by me. Artist's claim, artist's
voice. Blush. Captivation. Perfumed petunias. Snowdrops
of hope. Light-hearted shamrock. Rose, Austrian. Lovely.
Adoration, reverence, afterglow. Burning bush.

—Deborah Gerrish

Poem and Prompt

Superstition

Don't bathe in a thunderstorm,
my mother would say. Lightning

can strike. I think of this as
I watch from the tub, each flash,

a split-second closer to
my wife tapping on the door,

jimmying the lock when she
gets no answer, finding me

dead, body still warm and soft
against the white porcelain.

But nothing ever happens.
And I do not want to go,

not yet, not while water rolls
down the curves of my shoulders

in beads, not without raising
my hands in prayer, not until

I can pull back the curtain
satisfied that I am clean.

—Robert Fillman

The poet begins his poem with a single superstition. The speaker identifies the person who issued the warning and pinpoints the consequence of disregarding the warning. Then he zeroes in on his own disregarding as he bathes during a storm. He imagines the consequence: his wife finding him dead in the tub.

At the beginning of stanza 6, he introduces a turn with the word *But* and goes on to enjoy his bath unharmed. A turn, or reversal, in a poem ups the stakes and often brings in surprise.

The poem consists of five sentences with all but two lines enjambed. With one line tumbling into the next, we get a waterfall effect as the speaker's imagination takes flight.

If you read the poem aloud, you should notice the predominance of *er* sounds throughout: *thunderstorm, mother, closer, answer, ever, water, curves, shoulders, prayer, curtain.* This technique of sound repetition adds a subtle music to the poem.

✐ ✐ ✐

For your own superstition poem, first choose a superstition to work with. You might choose one of the following, but feel free to choose something not on this list:

> Don't step on a crack.
> Never walk under a ladder.
> If you spill salt, throw a pinch of it over your shoulder.
> Don't let a black cat cross your path.

(You can find additional superstitions by googling "common superstitions.")

Who gave you the warning? What consequence will supposedly ensue if the superstition is violated?

Now begin your draft with the superstition and the consequence. Imagine violating the superstition and what happens as a result. Work your thoughts into your draft.

Bring in your turn. Introduce it with a word or phrase such as *but, although, though, however, on the other hand, nevertheless, yet, still.*

Now bring in the joy of having broken the superstition. Write until you surprise yourself.

As you revise, work with enjambed lines instead of ones with terminal punctuation at line endings.

Read your draft aloud. Is there a sound that grabs your ear? Work in some repetition of that sound throughout the poem. This will necessitate some word changes. That's a good thing.

Sample Poems

Step on a Crack

Step on a crack, break your mother's back,
I learned from someone when a pre-school child.

How carefully I hopped from crumbling square to
square of the concrete sidewalk riddled with weeds,

saving my mother as we walked down the avenue
to the drugstore soda shop. I squashed many a small

bug while mother remained strong, her spine erect as
she pushed my baby sister's carriage across the pebbled

slabs. I remember those walks as I carefully navigate the
uneven stepping stones between me and the rest of the

world today, fearful of the cracks between them that would
fracture the already collapsing vertebrae of my own aging

spinal column. Mother died some twenty years ago from a
collision with an eighteen-wheeler, her back intact although

her ribs were shattered, lungs punctured, and heart bruised.
But she escaped the curse of any cracks I might have stepped

on over the years since I kept watch for them along the way,
hoping to protect us both, wearing this habit as if I were a nun,

convent walls a bulwark against our porous fragile bones,
eyes cast down as I chant this daily liturgy of protection.

—Penny Harter

Allergic Superstition

Truth be told, I'm the fool.
Truth be told, it's pine pollen,

spring air clogged with it, my skin
tingling as I sneeze and sneeze and sneeze.

But my mother says if your nose itches,
you'll kiss a fool

and who knows where that could lead?
Who would want to be led

anywhere by a fool? I would.
I would like to kiss you,

whoever you are, on both cheeks,
on your eyelids, the curve of your jaw, on your itchy, itchy nose.

I would like to kiss you full on the mouth.
Sensible sorts will call me a fool

for love, and they'll be right. I'll kiss
the top of your head, the tips of your fingers,

those ticklish parts my mother never mentions.
I will kiss you until you beg me

to stop, until you beg me for more.
So lead me astray, woo me

along that primrose path, brimming
with golden and lavender pollen,

sonorous with bees and chirping birds, which is how
we all got here in the first place.

—Lynn Domina

Bonus Prompts: Repetition

—J. C. Todd

1. Braiding the Words

To get started, quickly draft a poem about a favorite childhood toy. Now to braid sound and sense, rework the poem so that it repeats one or two words from the end of each line at the beginning of the next line, using those repeated words in a new context. Shift, for instance, from noun to verb, embed a repetition in a compound word, switch to a different word that is a close rhyme, or use a homonym to change the meaning but retain the sound.

Here's an example from my poem "Ornamental":

> However enticing a window's ornamental **fretting**,
> someone is **fretting** behind it about the **secret of herself**
> on a **shelf**, **secreted** away to keep her **safe**,
>
> a **keepsake** like those jewels, embroidered silks . . .

2. Rapid Repeats

At the top of a page, write two words, each one syllable. Repeat them, with variations, in the opening lines of a poem about the scent of someone's perfume or cologne. In subsequent lines, repeat different word pairs. Experiment with the following strategies: change the word's grammatical use; embed it in another word (*bell* in *bellow*); switch to a word that is a close rhyme; explore homonymic possibilities. Rapid repeats build momentum and urgency. Be inventive!

Here's an example from Catherine Wing's "A Small Psalm":

> Sorrow be gone, be a goner, be forsooth un-sooth, make like a
> suit and beat it, vamoose from the heavy heavy, be out from
> under the night's crawlspace, call not for another stone, more
> weight more weight, be extinguished, extinguish the dark . . .

3. Repetition and Rhythmic Pattern

In Joy Harjo's poem "She Had Some Horses," the poet sets up a drumbeat with her repetition of *She had some horses*. The poet adds variety with the addition of a clause that gets repeated: *She had horses who were bodies of sand. / She had horses who were maps drawn of blood.* And then she varies that pattern with the addition of a prepositional phrase: *She had horses with eyes of trains. / She had horses with full, brown thighs.* Change Harjo's opening words, e.g., *He had some dogs, They had some birds, She loved some lovers.* Then try your hand at using a rhythmic pattern. Repeat and vary.

VI. Figurative Language: Simile

When you lose yourself in your work,
and you feel at one with it, it is like love.

—Donald Hall

Craft Talk: It's Like This

—Danusha Laméris

The contract between the writer and the reader is a delicate thing. It requires the writer to lie, and the reader to believe the lie. Thus, the very basis of the relationship is tenuous. Furthermore, it takes place in the absence of the other, on the island of the page. And so we begin, separated at the start.

The art of writing is to construct a world in which the reader is granted an experience. One that, in poetry in particular, leads the reader to an expanded, shared moment, a new awareness that lives behind the language, just as an opening—or cave— might exist behind a waterfall.

Though, of course, that understanding isn't behind a waterfall, at all. It's only *like* that. Which is the purpose of the simile: to say this is and isn't what I'm trying to say. The choice between a simile and a metaphor often depends on how far we can push the lie.

The poem, "Not the Last," written by Ann Emerson shortly before she died, begins:

> In this story I am an old animal
> and not sad in the way people think
> about horses vanishing in the West.

The opening lines startle, and, through metaphor, posit a more extreme reality than *I am like an old horse.* And perhaps because of the poet's mortal authority, it works. She gets to claim any shapeshifting she wants, because she has the lived experience to do so. It would, in this case, weaken the poem had she done otherwise.

So, there is a gauge we can develop, a kind of personal measuring system, to determine whether the poem demands the authority, in a given moment, to go for the metaphor, or whether the poem requires the slight uncertainty of a simile. Or perhaps, it's more accurate to say, the liminal space the simile provides. It's not quite the thing we're saying, but close to it. As such, the simile can form either a nowhere land that allows the reader to float in a degree of uncertainty, or a bridge from one mode of perception to the next.

Consider Natalie Diaz's poem, "I Watch Her Eat the Apple": *The apple pulses like a red bird in her hand . . . / she bites, cleaving away a red wing.*

Somewhere in between the introductory image and the developed one, the apple goes from being birdlike, to being an actual bird. The simile manages any resistance we may have had to having such an image thrust upon us. In other words, it manages the lie of writing by allowing readers a space to accommodate their disbelief.

Much of craft involves such negotiation. If I say two things are similar, as long as there is no obvious imbalance in weight between the two, readers will likely go with me. If I try to say two things are, in fact, the same, I am pushing readers into a position and inviting them to push back.

In my poem "Iris" I describe the blue and yellow petal of a flower, placed between a woman's breasts, as being *a kind of book mark*, a way to hold the page of an erotic memory. I like when the likeness, or simile, mirrors the actual. In this case, a petal is visually similar to a bookmark.

There may be occasions when the poet wishes to venture into the wilds of hyperbole, perhaps pushing the limits of belief. And here too some skillfulness is required. I think of the poem "Fire" by Matthew Dickman, which depicts a bonfire with friends, one of whom is playing a banjo and is described as being *like an Appalachian Prince*. But it's the next bit that stays with me:

> The court surrounding him and the deer
> off in the dark hills like the French, terrified
> but in love and hungry.

From deer to military is a leap, for sure, but we arrive there, somewhere beyond our own imagining, as many a good poem leads us—one simile at a time.

Poem and Prompt

Rewinding an Overdose on a Projector

Blacker. Black. The foam drools back
up his chin, over his lips and behind his teeth.
The boy on the floor floats onto the bed.
Gravity returns. His hands twitch.
The heart wakes like a handcar pumping faster and faster
on its greased tracks. Eyes flick open.
Blood threads through a needle, draws into a tube.
The syringe handle lifts his thumb.
The hole in his vein where he left us seals.
The boy injects a liquid into the cotton
that drowns inside a spoon. He unties the leather belt
around his arm, pushes the sleeve to his wrist.
The wet cotton lifts, fluffs into a dry white ball.
The flame beneath the spoon shrinks to a spark,
is sucked inside the chamber where it grows cold,
then colder. The heroin bubbles to powder.
The water pours into a plastic bottle. The powder rains
into a vial where it sleeps like an only child.
All the contents on the bed spill into a bag.
The boy stands, feeds his belt through the loops.
This is where I snip the film and burn it.
What remains are the few hundred frames
reeling: the boy unlocking a bedroom door,
a black jacket rising from the floor, each sleeve
taking an arm like a mother and father.

       —Sean Shearer

The narrative action in this poem is reversed. Something horrible
has happened—a heroin overdose. As we all do after horrible
events, the speaker wishes to turn back the clock. Therefore, he

123

begins at the end of the story, reversing and undoing each action that led up to the overdose and its catastrophic conclusion.

Notice the declarative sentences with their article/subject/action verb construction, e.g., *The foam drools, The heart wakes, The boy injects*. Notice too the flat, lifeless tone that results from this syntax, ironically at odds with the use of the personal first-person speaker.

The imagery makes the scene one we can see. Much of the imagery results from the strong verbs: *Eyes flick open, Blood threads, The syringe handle lifts his thumb*. The poet forces us to see the scene. And because we see it, we feel it.

In lines 5, 18, and 25 the poet employs three powerful similes, each of which illustrates that sometimes a simile works better than a metaphor. In the closing simile, the speaker describes the boy's black jacket, *each sleeve / taking an arm like a mother and a father*. This closing simile makes our hearts ache for the boy and his parents.

The poet might have given more prominence to the actions by using stanzas, but he opted to use a single stanza which contributes to the poem's fast pace and the absence of the relief that stanza breaks might bring.

✎ ✎ ✎

For your own reverse action poem, first choose an event that had a negative outcome. This could be something you experienced, observed, or heard about from someone else. It could also be something you heard or read about in the news. Perhaps a dog getting killed by a car, a heart attack, a house fire.

Then make a list of actions leading up to the end. Put these actions in chronological order. This is just a list, not a draft.

Now beginning at the end of your list, draft your poem, ending with what's at the beginning of your list.

Use a first-person speaker.

Use declarative sentences. Use active and energetic verbs.

As you revise, work in some imagery and similes. Put your strongest simile at the end of the poem.

How does the single stanza work for your poem? Feel free to try a different format.

Commentary: The Function of Similes

—Sean Shearer

Although this poem is sparse in similes, the emotional weight of each one tends to be heavier the more the reader moves through the poem. The first one that appears is the heart being compared to the vehicle of the handcar as it wakes. Not much of an emotional weight, but it begins the poem's rhetorical structure of the body being this rickety vehicle for the subject. The next two similes are the opposite as they compare inanimate objects to a living thing. These similes are hermetically tied to family, i.e., only child, mother, and father.

"Rewinding an Overdose on a Projector" is about the practicalities of shooting up heroin, an ugly subject matter. When you have the amalgam of a family setting beneath the poem, it creates a much stranger and stronger emotional weight for the reader.

The last simile in the poem will always haunt me when I read it. The speaker is clutching these bodies that signify a balance or protection in life—a mother and a father—whereas we already know from the very beginning of the poem that the speaker can no longer be protected.

Sample Poems

Do Over

Like a cripple at a summer tent revival,
my sister rose from the ICU bed,
flicked off the ventilator,
removed IVs and tubes.
Her chest expanded with each breath.
Intracranial pressure decreased,
brain no longer a bruised melon.
Blood pressure stabilized.
Pupils responded to light.
Medevac helicopter blades reversed
direction, returned her to the road
that ran parallel to white water.
She eased back into her car, listened
to Paul Simon's *Graceland* spill
from the radio until the Mustang
rounded the blind curve,
passed her Subaru.
She then off-loaded her kayak,
slid into the rapids.

—Nina Bennett
published in *Cultural Daily*

Slow-Motion Reverse-Replay, Myocardial Infarction

Shards of crystal rise
from the terracotta floor, swirl
as if charmed by a wizard's circling wand.
They form the stem, then bowl
of last night's wineglass, which floats
to the counter
just as his heart starts again
like the slow wingbeat of a great heron,
its reliable lub dub, lub dub.
Purple bruises on his cheek fade,
rosiness returns, feet pulse with cozy blood.
His knees unbuckle. He rises.
Settles into his chair's knowing shape.

[Pause.
That's the stop-action I want
burnt on my retina.]

He's like a buoyant boy on a birthday,
lips pursed for the Bulldog kickoff,
a gruff *WOOF WOOF WOOF!*
He's glued to TV's pre-game pomp—
Georgia-Alabama—texting buddies,
Tide ain't gonna roll today!
The ambulance never needs to scream.
The house isn't skin-prickling quiet.
My key doesn't shake in the lock.
On the two-hour trip, my gut isn't sick,
my brain doesn't fast-talk—
his phone must be dead, his phone must be lost.
Instead, I waltz with the hairpin curves,
Cat Stevens singing "Morning Has Broken."
My heart stays with October's trees—
the red flags only their leaves.

—Karen Paul Holmes

Poem and Prompt

New Restrictions

It doesn't matter how many
Wallace Stevens poems you've memorized
or if you had sex in the graveyard
like an upside-down puppet
or painted your apartment red
so it feels like sleeping inside a heart
or the trees were frozen with ravens
which you sent pictures of to everyone you know
or your pie dough's perfect
or you once ran a sub-5-minute mile
or you're on the last draft
of your mystery novel and still
don't know if the vicar did it
or every morning that summer
you saw a fox stepping through the fog
but it got no closer
or once you helped drag a deer
off the road by the antlers
it blinked
or which song comes from which side
of your mouth as you drive
all night all night all night
or how deep and long you carry
a hitch in your breath after crying
or shot a man in Tennessee
or were so happy in France
or left your favorite scarf in a café,
the one with the birds and terrible art
or the Klimt
or you call your mother once a week
even after she's dead
or can't see a swan without panic
or have almost figured out
what happened to you as a child,

urge, urge, nothing but urge
or 600 daffodils
or a knife in the glove box
or a butterfly on a bell,
you can't park here.

—Dean Young

Young gives us a wonderful single-sentence poem. The poem consists of a long list of good acts which are not enough to allow the *you* who has done them to park in the newly restricted area. By withholding the restriction of the title until the end of the poem, the poet increases the poem's buildup, intensity, and expectation—an expectation which is foiled at the end as the restriction seems so small. This contrast adds a touch of humor.

In order to make a long one-sentence poem work, the poet relies on conjunctions to hold together the different items in the list. Note the abundance of the word *or*. The use of this conjunction removes the need for punctuation. That too adds to the speed of the poem. We can't stop to breathe.

Young includes some wonderful similes, e.g., the auditor who has *had sex in the graveyard / like an upside-down puppet* and the apartment painted red *so it feels like sleeping inside a heart.*

The poem is also filled with wonderful images—the trees *frozen with ravens,* the fox *stepping through the fog,* and the deer being dragged *off the road by the antlers.*

Notice the poet's fondness for things in groups of three. Lines 9, 10, and 11 all begin with *or.* That threesome is repeated two additional times, giving us three groups of three repetitions. We also have *all night all night all night* and *urge, urge, nothing but urge.*

Before you begin your one-sentence poem, choose a rule or restriction to use at the end of the poem, e.g., no smoking on the premises, lights out at 9, books must be returned on time, no cheating allowed, clean up after your dog.

Then begin your draft with *It doesn't matter* . . . and keep going with a long list of good deeds that won't allow the *you* of the poem to avoid compliance with the rule.

Connect the different items in your list with conjunctions: *and, but, if, for, nor, or, so, yet, because*. Focus on one conjunction so that you get the rhythm and repetition of Young's poem.

Address the second-person *you* throughout the poem.

Use lots of images and a few similes.

Challenge yourself to work with groupings of three.

When revising, go back to the beginning of your poem and reword the first line.

Sample Poems

Warning

It doesn't matter if you're the god
of the door-to-door
or if choosing between
apples and oranges makes you sexually
confused or if time slows down
as it gets closer
to earth's mass and you're in a lab
trying to come up with a "moister brownie"
or if you're waiting for the cut-glass river
to shatter so you have something
to eat and love like snow blindness
afflicts you and says it will show you
a bridge of limbs that you can
cross, that you can virtually feel
in this filthy November with your
dimestore necklace and house of corrections
hair without ever learning how to zigzag
through a cocktail party or that
simoom means a hot, poisonous wind
in Arabic or that he's left
so many times, you no longer believe
in object permanence
and when you cried into his crow-
shined hair, inside your hallowed
chambers, you felt a coin
in your gullet and someone else's
life flashed before your eyes as if
you had been a flight risk or the dark
clearing its throat or a night that
came in like a drunk uncle imagining
he's home for good
or that you were frozen
in the crosshairs
of a tornado that would make you want

to crawl back inside
your mother who
sits on the New York Public Library
steps where it says for your own safety
do not climb
on the lions.

—Cathy Colman

Of the Eternal Waters

I don't care
if you saved a little boy
by grabbing the tail of his shirt
as he was falling off a Ferris wheel
or performed a Heimlich
as Danny choked on chicken
or tucked your feet behind your neck
and balanced on your hands
or if you loved to snuggle
with your blue-eyed roundish mother
or you loved your Army father
but couldn't make his slide rule work
or you wish you had a parrot
who said *timor mortis conturbat me*
or you wish you had an Airedale
or you wish you had a kitten
or your son painted your bedroom
so it's like sleeping in a daffodil
or your apple pie's to die for
or you once ate a pansy
and mustard and potato chips
and applesauce on tuna
or you dream you could wander
on every glorious *Wanderweg*
in the flower-speckled Alps
or your irises are blooming
or your salvias are blooming
or something ate your basil
or Van Gogh, Magritte, and Brueghel
or one night by the Seine
or one noon in the café
or you love his warm, blunt hands
or fire glints off your opal ring
or you've taught here thirty years
or your smile could charm a badger
you can't wade in this fountain.

—Ann Fisher-Wirth

Bonus Prompts: Simile

—Catherine Doty

1. Describing with Similes

My uncle's eyebrows are like two caterpillars kissing.
My uncle's eyebrows are like the Earth's tectonic plates shifting.
My uncle's eyebrows are like two fuzzy black slippers.
They're as wiggly as a box full of puppies.

The lines above capture, with similes, one small part of a whole person. Choose one specific thing about yourself or another person, perhaps the feet, singing voice, ears, or eyes. Then write as many similes about it as you can. Now rev up your imagination and write more. It's when you think you have nothing else to say that the freshest, newest, most surprising observations will come to you. Go for twenty similes or more, and make them as different from each other as you can. Now turn your litany of similes into a poem.

2. Old Story in New Similes

Choose a familiar story that most people will know, such as Little Red Riding Hood or Frankenstein. Or choose one incident from a book you love, e.g., Harry Potter meets Moaning Myrtle. Or choose a story your family likes to tell over and over again, e.g., driving to the hospital in a snow storm when you were about to be born. Write the story as a narrative poem, making it richer and more interesting with similes.

3. Creating Voice with Similes

Write in the voice of an animal or an object describing something it saw a human do. Try to put yourself in the animal or object's place, to think and feel like your subject. Begin with description, then bring in inventive and interesting similes to capture what the subject thinks and feels. Here are a few examples of what you might write about: your dog sits in the back seat as you drive, a cat watches kids playing outside the window, the antique vase thinks about its life on the shelf.

VII. Figurative Language: Metaphor

I have hidden behind the beauty of metaphors . . .

—C. Dale Young

Craft Talk: Metaphor as Lowrider

—Jan Beatty

Not a self-conscious leap, but the organic, elemental journey in. How to write a metaphor? I would say like one writes at 4 AM in the midst of a dream—without thinking too much. Turn off your high mind and go.

Write: *the eye as telescope the wanderer the eye as drill as gemstone, now red and channeling.*

Let words follow each other in a list of not-so-stellar metaphors—yet. And, here we are: more inside the life of another thing or being, through the dreamscape, through the willingness to write the so-called ordinary. Why is everyone afraid to write lists of words as they fall, stumbly, out of us? Of course, because of the hyper-vigilant internal censor, ready to chop, shred, and bulldoze. Here's a metaphor for you: the censor is a fraidy cat with dreams of a cleaver.

Granted, the mysterious eye can take us many places, and many of them are cliché. So what? If you're not willing to write the dreadful, the sad, limp metaphor—how will you find the diving figure in all its shining?

The proof: in two short lines of not lifting the pen (this should be a pen on paper, not the computer), we've come upon a drill bit, which could be a violent leap from the eye; a gemstone channeling in and down into the body, on fire. We have stepped inside. Now something is changing.

The metaphor in its leaping *allows*, gives immediate transport. I like to think of it as a long diving board from the inner qualities of a word—off into the air—then possibly landing. In its allowing, it catapults us immediately into another zone (air) and deeper (water), quickly.

If the leaping goes haywire, as in an unsuccessful metaphor, it can take us not inward, deeper—but thrash us out of the poem, away from any elemental sense of the word, the thing.

Sometimes this thrashing can happen with the overzealous metaphor, running with the conscious mind into self-consciously clever places: *The eye is now a brown suitcase*.

Yes, a leap, but distracting. And the suitcase feels very *human-made*—not *born*, not of the elemental body. You could argue that telescope is the same in its *thing-ness*, yet the obvious replicated shape, the lens, the seeing carries it as a possible, though uninspired metaphor. The suitcase feels heavy, shut down, contained—whereas the eye is floating, liquidy.

A property or a linked association must spring between the tenor and the vehicle of the metaphor and make it hum like an engine.

The tenor is like the word-body, and the vehicle is the car you climb in to make the metaphor run. And who wants to psychically climb into a dependable, boring, reasonable car—when you can jump into a pitch black V-8 Charger with a hemi? Or a lowrider gliding *low and slow* then pumping up and down? The hydraulics of language. Front and rear wheels, *juiced all around*. Who wouldn't want that?

> My heart is a lowrider, my blood
> flames the side panels. Circle
> the town square, I'm burning
> you awake.

I'm feeling it. I'm inside it. It's no longer a metaphor. It's transformation. I'm all in.

Poem and Prompt

I Am Pamela Pan

He ran away the day he was born, after
hearing us discussing what a fine man
he would be. We never saw him again.
I do not know his face. I've lost my shadow.

I learn about him from the mockingbirds,
how he lived with fairies in Kensington Gardens.
But he is not a lost boy, he knows where he is.
He chose a different way, the *second* to the right.

The birds say red hair, green rags, flight like a finch's.
They cannot tell me if he has my husband's chin,
as I suspect, or his able hands. My boy can never know
I am the green in his eyes, and I tell fine stories.

He's the towel I cry into when the hanky's too small.
He is my straight on till morning, every night.
He will never grow up or get bored. He will never marry.
Instead, he is "youth and joy," he tells Hook, "a little bird

that has broken out of the egg." I'm the shattered shell,
in irretrievable pieces, a droughtland of shards.
I had more children, daughters, thankfully—
they tend to stay around. I am afraid to tell them

I lost their brother, they'll think me careless.
But one can't hold back a magic wish, especially
when it wants to share itself. One can't grasp glee
and mischief. It's easier to grab hold of a minute ago.

Here in Alwaysland, the taxes and maids must be paid,
the dinners earned and cleaned up, the corners tucked.
The stories repeat themselves, the births, the funerals.
Perhaps he was right to go. I miss him so.

—Tina Kelley

141

In this persona poem the first-person speaker poses as Pamela Pan, the newly created mother of Peter Pan, made famous in the story by J. M. Barrie. As we read, we learn things about Peter that we did not know before. More importantly, we learn the story from a mother's point of view. No longer is the story one of adventure, of a boy's fantasy in Neverland. Now it's the story of a mother who has lost her child and lives in *Alwaysland*, a new country where grief never ends.

What Pamela knows about Peter's life she learns from the mockingbirds. As she learns via this invention, so too do we. The story of Peter as we know it enlarges. We learn that Peter ran away the day he was born—a nice bit of hyperbole—because he overheard his parents mapping out his life.

The story is further enlarged by contrast. While Peter lives in a world of fantasy, Pamela lives in a world where taxes must be paid, dinners earned, and household chores completed.

Kelley gives us a series of poignant declarative sentences: *We never saw him again. / I do not know his face. / I've lost my shadow*. Notice especially the sentence that closes the poem: *I miss him so*, a sentence that hits hard with its simplicity and starkness.

Notice the metaphors that the poet uses to express grief. For example, Pamela says that Peter is her missing *shadow* and the *towel I cry into when the hanky's too small*, while she is *the shattered shell*. These metaphors are more effective than plain statement and descriptive details of her sorrow would be.

Finally, notice the formal pattern Kelley uses to contain her poem's emotional story. She gives us seven four-line stanzas with fairly even line lengths.

/ / /

For your own persona poem, select an unknown or lesser known relative of a character in a well-known piece of literature, one that readers are likely to be familiar with. For example, you might choose Cinderella's stepsister or the husband of the witch in the Hansel and Gretel story. You might instead invent a new character to insert into the known story, for example, Gatsby's housekeeper or his former fiancée.

Using first-person point of view and speaking as your chosen character, begin your draft. Consider how the life of the main character affected your character's life. Provide a limited number of well-chosen details. Make references to the known story, but focus on filling us in on what is not already known.

Work in a contrast.

Use some stark declarative sentences.

Sprinkle your draft with metaphors. Zero in on the best ones and discard the less effective ones.

Impose a formal structure on your draft.

Commentary: Persona Poem as Opportunity

—Tina Kelley

My father always loved the work of J. M. Barrie, and when I finally got around to reading *Peter Pan*, I enjoyed the chance to explore the original Peter, not the Disney version. I made a note to write a dramatic monologue by his mother, and this poem emerged, a month after the death of my dad, actually—*the towel I cry into when the hanky's too small* is definitely from that period.

There are so many characters in literature we never hear from, though it's never too late to fix that. Often, they are women. I think of Goldilocks' mother, who never taught the girl boundaries and probably had an aneurysm when she first read that fairy tale. For that matter, name one mom left breathing in Disneyland. Orphaned: Bambi, Cinderella, Snow White. Scraping by with just dad: Belle, Jasmine, Ariel. Sent to inadequate foster care: Sleeping Beauty and Simba. Peter Pan's mother had effectively lost her son forever, yet he was still so very alive somewhere. I found her very compelling.

Peter's story is rich with imagery, some of it familiar, and I figured hers should be too. His shadow becomes an object his sister sews back on. He dwells in the stars, *second to the right, straight on till morning*. When I imagined Peter in Kensington Gardens, I compared his flight to a finch's motion, which always reminds me of the wires between utility poles. He is youth and joy and a hatchling.

But a bereaved mother would be the opposite—that dry dirt surrounding the cracks in *droughtland*. There must be a specific word for those cracks, but it would be too technical, and I figured *shards* fit well with *shattered* and *shell*—never say no when the alliteration muse smiles upon you! As I became the newly named Pamela Pan, I had to invent her life. I inhabited her body, her life, her voice. I became her voice. That was the fun and the challenge of writing this persona poem.

A persona poem, especially one about a literary character, can provide a full raft of raw materials for making metaphors, both from the original story and your own imagination. Play around with them—may they never grow old!

Sample Poems

Elegy for Goliath

> *David prevailed over Goliath . . . grasped*
> *Goliath's sword . . . cut off his head.*
> —I Samuel 17. 50,51

Victors write the histories. The Israelites wrote his story. Let this be Goliath's truth. He was my brother. He was no giant or freak of nature, but tall and strong, a powerful man. We wept the day he left our village, left the flocks he loved to tend, left our father, left his children, left his home that was his life. He was simple, no match for guile. He believed his generals who called him champion, could not see they abused his strength. Goliath with his hands like boulders, my brother with his sword of light, a javelin of death across his back, covered in bronze along his height. The generals taught him he was invincible and sent him into the valley of death. They called him their anointed one, set apart, a nation's glory. He thought to fight another champion, not another nation's god. When he fell, his army fled. He died in the dust, a soldier alone, innocent of all but duty. Honor him for his power and promise. Pity him, a holy fool.

—Jane Mary Curran

Sarabelle Crusoe

We were married secretly
because his parents
wanted him to study law
but Robinson was called

to find his fortunes by sea.
I've been waiting now five years
caring for the twins
he cannot know exist.

I'd begged him not to go.
The sea was an enemy—
shipwreck was the devil's pitchfork
that had stabbed my own father.

In the end, his parents
have taken me in as a drudge
scrubbing their muddied floors
wringing out their smelly laundry

yet I'm grateful that they are
willing grandparents to Ivy
and Allan—well-fed
and cherished. But I need

a husband to be my gentle breeze.
The world assumes he's dead
but no, he cannot be whisked away
forever. I picture him

as lord of a magical island
where trees bend in homage
offering ripe fruits to his lips.
Barley and rice sprout

at the beckon of his fingers.
Fire sparks at the command
of flint he's extricated
from breakaway planks.

I watch for each time a ship
stands upon the horizon
I rush with the children
to the pier and wait.

Will this be the day
of all our rescues?

—Charlotte Mandel

Poem and Prompt

How to Swallow an Elephant

Place an old photo of your father face up in a saucer of milk.

Make a list
of all the mistakes you own.

Tattoo it in red ink across both wrists.

Count the times you screamed yourself awake behind the wheel

or left an emergency room with only stitches.

Your father's absence
fuels your passion to be present.

Put it at the beginning of a list of gifts from him.

Take your own children home to the projects.

Let them play in the dirt where your anger was born.

Make the longer journey to his perfect front lawn.

Introduce him as their grandfather.
Stay long enough for one of you to touch.

      —Frank X Walker

Instruction poems are often facile and frivolous, but Walker's has substance. The elephant in the title reveals itself to be a metaphor for the speaker's father. But can an elephant be swallowed? Of course not, so this figure is also an example of hyperbole. As we read the poem, we begin to suspect that the speaker is really talking about something else that is hard to swallow—forgiveness. Although the poet gives us sparse details, we are able to piece together a story of abandonment. That abandonment meant a hard life for the speaker while the father went off to live in comfort. This subject matter is the opposite of facile and frivolous.

The instruction approach seems ideal for this poem. Its step-by-step process creates distance, a cool tone, and a touch of irony as it suggests control while anger simmers beneath the surface. The use of imperative sentences additionally implies control as the second-person *you* is told what to do. Consider how the tone would change if the poet spoke as *I*.

Notice the steps the poet lists. The opening line is odd, enigmatic. But right in the middle of it, there's the elephant. What happens to a photo placed in a saucer of milk?

The speaker then asks the *you* to make the first of two lists, this one of mistakes the *you* has made. This list is to be tattooed across both wrists in red ink, a powerful image suggesting the possibility of suicide.

Later comes the direction to make a second list, this one of gifts from the father. We suspect that this will be a short list.

We learn that the speaker now has children of his own and that he grew up in the projects where his anger was born. The dirt where he played as a child is contrasted with the *perfect front lawn of the father*.

✎ ✎ ✎

For your instruction poem, choose an elephant of your own to get rid of. What burden have you been carrying around? Consider how you might get rid of it or tame it or forget it. Keep it personal and uncomfortable. Create a metaphor for the subject of your poem, e.g., is it a boulder that needs to be smashed, a sour pickle that must be consumed, a rotten molar that must be extracted? Give your poem a "how to" title.

Begin with a quirky line. Then one by one, give the steps in your instructions. Use imperative sentences and second-person point of view; direct the instructions to a *you*.

Try to achieve the ironic tone of Walker's poem. Keep the anger and the passion under the surface. Use understatement and indirection.

Let the images do some work for the poem. Let them express the emotion and hint at the story behind the emotion.

Sample Poems

How to Set a Squirrel Free

Keep the letter he wrote from rehab,
the only apology you will ever get.

Or cut it up into a collage. Burn the collage.
Mix the ashes with coffee grounds

to feed the hydrangea. If you like that sort of thing.
Big blue flowers can cover a lot of torn-up ground.

Flirt with the coffee guy. Or the contractor
replacing the sheetrock you tried to patch
after he punched the wall. Also the dog.

List the ways you protected your bank account
and credit cards: fraud and theft can come from
inside the house.

Don't tally up the money spent on suspended
licenses, lawyers, liquor. Don't imagine spending it

instead on rent, groceries, vacation.
Don't even think about snorkeling.

Fold the protective order, cottony soft and limp from
being carried in your pocket, into an origami crane.

Don't burn that. Hang it as a Christmas ornament.
Put it in the window every year like a Yahrtzeit candle.

When your little girl gets out of bed because she can't sleep
and she's afraid of the noise the branches make against the house,

tell her a silly story full of cute animals caring for each other.
Tell her not to wait for a knight to save her; he's weighted down
trapped inside all that heavy armor.

—Elizabeth S. Wolf

How to Make a Paper Heart

Never put down a stencil and always stick to your gut.
If your scissors are dulled, no matter. In fact, that's better.

Make each cut a cigarette burn on carpet, the blistered
sting of a Wild Turkey slug. For fun, try shutting your eyes.

Let the blades find their pattern the way an outstretched hand might
slide fingers over objects in the dark. Read impressions

on everything you touch, that plush-stuffed unicorn with its
        one glass eye still able to watch, a Zippo lighter drained
of luck. Decorate with those split ends tucked behind your ears,

fringes from a faded pair of denim shorts, the curling
whiskers of a man that came and left without the caution

of a hunter's silence. Save each scrap that falls. Use every
part. Think how all those pieces might be the embroidery

on a nightie your lover delicately lifts over
your head, tosses to the floor. Reds and pinks are always nice—

—Robert Fillman

Poem and Prompt

My Invisible Horse and the Speed of Human Decency

People always tell me, "Don't put the cart
before the horse," which is curious
because I don't have a horse.
Is this some new advancement in public shaming—
repeatedly drawing one's attention
to that which one is currently not, and never
has been, in possession of?
If ever, I happen to obtain a Clydesdale,
then I'll align, absolutely, it to its proper position
in relation to the cart, but I can't
do that because all I have is the cart.
One solitary cart—a little grief wagon that goes
precisely nowhere—along with, apparently, one
invisible horse, which does not pull,
does not haul, does not in any fashion
budge, impel or tow my disaster buggy
up the hill or down the road.
I'm not asking for much. A more tender world
with less hatred strutting the streets.
Perhaps a downtick in state-sanctioned violence
against civilians. Wind through the trees.
Water under the bridge. Kindness.
LOL, says the world. *These things take time*, says
the Office of Disappointment. *Change cannot
be rushed*, says the roundtable of my smartest friends.
Then, together, they say, *The cart!*
They say, *The horse!*
They say, *Haven't we told you already?*
So my invisible horse remains
standing where it previously stood:
between hotdog stands and hallelujahs,
between the Nasdaq and the moon's adumbral visage,
between the status quo and The Great Filter,
and I can see that it's not his fault—being

invisible and not existing—
how he's the product of both my imagination
and society's failure of imagination.
Watch how I press my hand against his translucent flank.
How I hold two sugar cubes to his hypothetical mouth.
How I say I want to believe in him,
speaking softly into his missing ear.

—Matthew Olzmann

Olzmann begins his poem with a maxim, one so often said that it's become a cliché. Thus, he does what we're told not to do. He then uses the cliché to impel the poem forward. He gets away with this by creating a credulous speaker who takes the cliché literally. This strategy adds humor, especially as the naiveté is in stark contrast to the poet's command of language as seen in such lines as *repeatedly drawing one's attention / to that which one is currently not, and never / has been, in possession of.*

The speaker ambles on about his possible horse and cart and then stuns us with the metaphor of *a little grief wagon*, soon followed by another, *my disaster buggy*. Because the poet uses metaphors sparingly, the ones he does use become more important.

About midway through the poem, we find the insertion of a list of the speaker's simple desires. The list is followed by the reasons why the speaker can't have what he wants according to the *Office of Disappointment* and the *roundtable of my smartest friends*

Notice as the poem proceeds how the poet slips in contemporary language, e.g., *LOL*, the *Nasdaq*, and *The Great Filter*. Notice also the three parallel prepositional phrases: *between hotdog stands and hallelujahs, / between the Nasdaq and the moon's adumbral visage, / between the status quo and The Great Filter*. Parallelism appears again in the closing lines of the poem which contain a series of phrases beginning with *how*.

For your own poem, first select a maxim to work with. Here's a list of possibilities:

> Take the tiger by the tail.
> Do not look a gift horse in the mouth.
> Don't throw out the baby with the bathwater.
> Don't put all your eggs in one basket.
> Don't count your chickens before the eggs are hatched.
> Don't cry over spilled milk.
> Born with a silver spoon in his mouth.
> The grass is always greener on the other side.
> If you lie down with dogs, you get up with fleas.

To get started, borrow Olzmann's starter phrase: *People always tell me*_____. Insert your maxim in the blank space. Let yourself be a naïve speaker by taking the maxim literally. Keep going.

Along the way generate a small handful of relevant metaphors and plug the best ones into the poem.

Manage to work in a list of desires that seem relevant to your poem. Then include the reasons why the speaker can't have what he wants.

Work in some contemporary language, perhaps some tech terms.

Work in some parallel phrases.

End with tenderness.

As you revise, feel free to alter the pattern. If any parts of your draft aren't working kindly for the poem, remove those parts.

Consider if your poem works best as one long stanza or if it would work better broken into multiple stanzas.

Sample Poems

This dumb thing

My grandma has been telling me this dumb thing
since my drug sister died—when life gives you lemons
make lemonade—but I like lemons plain
the crayon yellow, their fisted feel
my sour smile, the pulp squeaking my teeth
and shouldn't my grandma know by now
life doesn't give? I'm a kid with no lemons
or cash, so one night at Food Lion
while Mom stares at the ramen
I scoot to the produce, shove two in my training bra
stick two more down my pants at my hips, walk
back to Mom like a penguin, drop two more
in the nest of her hoody, she feels lumps
at her neck but not until she's driving
then screams at my face for not wearing baggier clothes.

Home. You know how they say on TV
hey, kids, don't try this at home, well, I do
and true, it's a mess, the dull knife, the sugar
the ants, and the lemonade sucks
so when Grandma mentions this lemon/lemonade thing yet again
on my sister's should-a-been graduation
I grab a red magic marker, write the word three times
in giant font LEMONS LEMONS LEMONS
slice the letters with scissors, scrabble them on the linoleum
until they're not lemons. MOLE on the LOOSE
NEON NOEL! It's a flickering sign, my own SOS
I MOO and COO with its beat, I'm a LOON
I'm NO ONE, SOMEONE, all this MONEE in my hands.

LOOM. Now, there's a word you can use.
My sister and me made some potholders once
worthless until she stitched them onto her jean jacket—pockets—
and if I had a loom, I'd weave a dress with my mom's and dad's

and the moon's blue sadness, a tent dress, a sack dress
with pockets for the lemons I'm gonna keep stealing.

We're chameleons, I tell you, and when the doorbell rings
it won't be a tired cop—it'll be all the world's lemons
bright and ripe and begging to be made
into anything but
lemonade.

—Jenny Hubbard

Owls Mean Death

Beware the hoot-hoot of an owl at night,
the messenger who brings news of death—
that's what my grandmother told me

long before a great horned owl attacked
me in the cemetery, broad daylight
and next to her parents' tombstones.

I asked the Cherokee medicine man
why this happened, and he gave me
tobacco to pray with, to save

me from that curse, from beings
who walk in darkness and kill.
But at a gourd dance I saw

a man wearing an owl feather
in his cowboy hat, with powers
of that creature who flies between

day and night, who visits spirits
and returns with their songs,
some of them from my relatives,

ones who wait across the veil
for the eternal time when all of us
join in the same starlit dance.

—Denise Low

Bonus Prompts: Metaphor

—Joy Gaines-Friedler

1. Turning the Abstract into the Concrete

Make a list of abstract nouns. In a parallel column, make a list of concrete nouns. Try for a minimum of six in each column. For example:

Love	tiger
Friendship	dagger
Jealousy	peony

Then make metaphors by pairing up an abstract noun with a concrete one. For example, *Jealousy is a tiger*. Or *Love is a dagger*. Let that metaphor be your title or first line. Pick up and keep going.

2. Borrowing from the World

Look around you, read the newspaper, watch the news. Keep a list of scenes to use as metaphors. Write a poem in which the title is the literal subject, e.g., Divorce, Miscarriage, Getting Fired. Do not use this word or term in the poem itself. Instead, develop the poem with a description of a scene of something entirely different but equal in emotional impact. For example, a bird stunned on the patio after flying headfirst into the glass could be a metaphor for the shock of finding yourself divorced. A barn bursting into flame might show the agony of grief after a miscarriage.

3. The Metaphorical Love Poem / Curse Poem

Write a love poem to someone or something, even a body part. Build the poem with as many good metaphors as you can think of. Pile them on. Be extravagant in your praise of what is loved. Only mention the subject of the poem in the first line and again at the end.

Or try a curse poem directed towards someone or something you intensely dislike. Again, this could be a body part. Fill the poem with fiery metaphors. Be extravagant in your condemnation or hated of the subject. Only mention the subject of the poem in the first line and again at the end.

VIII. Figurative Language: Personification

Poetry is a way of taking life by the throat.

—Robert Frost

Craft Talk: The Humanizing Power of Personification

—Meg Kearney

Without thinking about it, people use personification in their speech every day: fires rage, clouds look angry, love is blind, popular books fly off shelves, and some cities never sleep. It seems we are always projecting our own emotions and actions onto inanimate objects and intangible concepts as a way to understand, convey, or connect with the otherwise mysterious, unknowable other. Personification helps us concretize the abstract and enable our listeners or readers to understand what we're trying to say, see what we see, feel what we feel. If a poem states, *Books were her only companions; / the only voices that whispered in her ear / were those that dwelled between pages / fragile and pale as her hands,* the emotional impact is much deeper than if it simply said, *She was lonely and not physically strong.*

Personification is a literary device that might date back to our days of telling stories around a campfire in the family cave, when perhaps rocks had eyes and trees spoke. We do know that in *The Epic of Gilgamesh,* our oldest surviving written story, *the finger of blessing / stretched out in mourning*, and a river and a mountain weep. In the 17th century Shakespeare vowed that death would never *brag* that his love *wander'st in his shade.* Around the same time John Donne wrote, *Death be not proud.* A couple hundred years later, Emily Dickinson called autumn's killing frost *the blonde assassin,* and in the 20th century Robert Hayden declared, *Night is an African juju man / weaving a wish and a weariness together.* Now in the 21st century, Li-Young Lee has described a childhood when *The photographs whispered to each other / from their frames in the hallway. / The cooking pots said your name / each time you walked past the kitchen.*

These examples are vibrant and memorable because they are fresh, new figures that haven't been overused—at least, that was the case when they were first penned. Poems fail when their figures are dead on arrival, like those *raging fires* referred to previously. When employing a tool like personification, it is the task of the poet to *make it new*, as Ezra Pound advised. While writers should not get hung up on the task of making everything sound completely original in their messy first drafts, one of their first tasks in the revision process should be to identify every place where language gets lazy and figures have, to use a clichéd personification, one foot in the grave.

Personification plays a role in strengthening the poem's argument or intent, and deepening the reader's understanding of and connection with it. Personification has the power to draw upon the senses—*the furnace wheezes like a drenched lung*, writes Cornelius Eady in "Handymen." It has the power to concretize and clarify the abstract—*solitude / Makes another gloomy entry / In its ledger, misery / Borrows another cup of rice*, says Charles Simic in "Breasts." And personification has the power to form connections that otherwise might prove weak or non-existent—a coconut is a *rough impenetrable / skull* in Chloe Martinez's "Kerala." When we use personification in our poems or in our speech, we often mean to compliment and/or honor our main subject: so we have Mother Nature and Father Time, and every ship's a she. But its main attraction and strength is the fact that if the poem is to recreate emotion and experience on the page, it is often best off appealing to what the reader knows best: what it is to be human.

Some claim that poetry is the path to world peace, as it enables us to appreciate each other's humanity and shows us how people of different cultures or backgrounds have more in common than not. Personification humanizes abstract concepts and seemingly foreign objects, customs, and ideas, thus cultivating understanding and empathy. Used skillfully and in moderation, this powerful device awakens the senses and weaves memorable connections in the reader's mind.

Poem and Prompt

Hunt

My heart, all night, knocks
   against my ribs,
claiming suffocation,

claustrophobia, and how
   it hates the dark.
A week, I've barely slept,

and when I do, I dream
   it's out—wet lump,
amphibious, blinking up

from a puddle on the floor, dull
   as a stewed tomato.
For hours now, I've shush-

shushed my jittered heart
   as if it were
a pet afraid of thunder,

a magician's snare roll
   I'm trying to slow
to adagio. But it

wants none of this, rabbits
   at the faucet's drip,
keeps claiming there's a dog,

nose down, who set it
   running in the womb,
a hound it can't outpace

if it must carry me,
   and carry me,
the way it has till now.

   —David O'Connell

In this poem of personification, the heart is given human attributes. It *knocks, claims*, and *hates*. The first-person speaker is the owner of this heart.

The poet uses the literary device of the dream to let his heart out of his body. Now he can see it and study it. Notice the lovely similes used to describe the heart: it's *dull / as a stewed tomato*, and it behaves *as if it were / a pet afraid of thunder*.

The personification resumes as the exposed heart speaks, claiming there's a dog chasing it. It would run but is weighed down by the speaker's body. The poet's use of personification adds a touch of irony as an organ of the human body becomes like a human.

Notice the poet's frequent use of monosyllabic words and the occasional insertion of a multi-syllabic word, such as *suffocation, claustrophobia*, and *adagio*. Read the poem aloud and hear how this alternation between monosyllabic and multi-syllabic words affects rhythm.

✐ ✐ ✐

For your personification poem, first choose a body part, e.g., tongue, ear, liver, appendix. Jot down some human characteristics of that organ. What does your body part do that a human does?

Generate a list of similes, e.g., *The tongue is like*_____.
My appendix is as useless as _____.
My ear looks like _____.

Using a first-person speaker, begin your draft. Introduce the body part right away. Continue to write quickly about it, bringing in its characteristics from your first list and the similes from your second list. Other characteristics and similes may arise organically. Welcome them in.

As you move to your next draft, pay attention to your diction. Try to alternate a series of monosyllabic words with an occasional multi-syllabic word.

Find an attractive format for your poem.

Sample Poems

A Mind at Home with Itself

My brain is always complaining as it crawls toward
     El Dorado, eyes upturned waiting for a lightning storm
to stun it speechless. But the sky never claps

open and there is no silence. Its knees bleeding,
     mouth running, my brain doesn't hear the alarm go off
in the morning, forgets to cancel its gym membership

even though it stopped going years ago. I have no choice
     but to ignore my brain. Walk to the other side
of the street when I see it. Stop answering its whiny

voicemails. I have a vision during a massage of my brain
     glistening like raw hamburger meat on the pavement
below a flashing motel sign. The meat turns

to blue glitter slime the neighborhood kids
     sell for fifty cents a bag that smells like cotton candy.
I steal a bag because it's my brain, after all, and toss it

on the kitchen counter. My brain is petrified I'm going
     to throw it away and begs for mercy. I pick it up,
slap it on the table, pound it, then ooze it between

my fingers. It feels smooth and cold and reassuring. I knead it
     a little longer before I throw it in the trash. My hands
are stained blue, glitter flecks my clothes, but finally, silence.

       —Marcia LeBeau
       published in *New Ohio Review*

In the Brief Inverted Room of My Fractured Ankle

I put my faith in the space between tibia
and talus, inside the filaments of ligament

torn and held sacred on a pillow like a small

god. In the hollows of chairs and under
cats, I place my faith, painworn, a litany

of deniability and binge. Twist-wakened

painspeak, one foot inversion booted
for weeks. In the all-too-brief clock time

angle me into special relativity, photon bounce

me slant, one billion times a second, stretch
time literally straightening lateral malleolus

combing ligament worsted smooth. I faith

you whole, holy, wholly healed, my ankle
my rock, my balanced foundation.

—Ronda Piszk Broatch

Poem and Prompt

The Disappointment of the Cantaloupes

Why do cantaloupes wish to resemble the moon
when, after all, they are filled with seeds, with sweet flesh?
When, after all, they grow along the earth and do not partake
of space, the freezing altitudes the moon moves within?
Why are they not content to be as they are: sunset-hued
beneath their grooved rinds? Instead, they admire the moon,
its cold, withholding demeanor, the pocked face that seems
ground from dry bone. The moon is lonely despite its grandeur,
while melons roll in beds of dirt and wish to burn nightly
with the glow of the sun. They are undone by human fingers,
by knives and teeth—not so the moon. The melons linger
in dusky fields, haunted by flies, tied by tangled vines
to soil. They are weighed down by their role: to multiply
themselves, thus to multiply sorrow—giving nourishment
to blackbirds and wolves, to antelope, insects, children.

—Dara Yen Elerath

Elerath begins her poem with three questions. At the same time,
she personifies the cantaloupes—they envy and admire the moon
and feel discontented. She describes and praises the fruit.

In line 6 the poem turns as we move to statements about the
moon. It too is personified, e.g., it has a *pocked face* and is
lonely. The speaker describes and praises the moon. Then she
contrasts her two items. By the end of the poem, we understand
that both fruit and moon are complex, each a mixture of virtues
and defects.

The poet uses a variety of sound devices. She uses some repetition:
after all, when, why. She also uses assonance as in this string
of *o* sounds: *bone, lonely, roll, glow, so, role, sorrow*; and this

string of *uh* sounds: *sun, undone, multiply*. We also find a good deal of alliteration: *bone, beds, burn; seeds, sweet, space; ground, grandeur, glow*. Finally, there's some internal rhyme: *cold* and *withholding, multiply* and *why, sun* and *undone, linger* and *fingers*.

✎ ✎ ✎

Let's write a poem of envy. First, select a fruit, vegetable, or flower. Then choose something from a different sphere as the object of envy. Both items should have some qualities in common, e.g., size, shape, color. Perhaps the cucumber envies the oak tree, the Concord grape envies the amethyst, the rose envies the beetle. Before you begin your draft, make a list of pieces of information or descriptive phrases about each item.

Begin your draft focusing on the first item. Ask a series of three questions in which you personify the item by giving it some human characteristics. Then praise the item and reveal its source of envy or disappointment.

Around line 6, shift your attention from the first to the second item. Point out its negative features but also include its virtues. As you proceed, contrast the two items, ultimately revealing the complex nature of both.

As you revise your poem, capitalize on some devices of sound. Include some repetition, assonance, alliteration, and internal rhyme.

Can you come up with a rhyme as wondrous as *cantaloupe* and *antelope*?

Commentary: Personification as Energizer

—Dara Yen Elerath

This poem began with the impulse to write something based on a question that personified its subject matter. I drafted several pieces using this approach, playing with different questions each time, *Why is the sea so angry?* for example, or *Why are stones so mute?* Writing in this imaginative fashion gives me the freedom to express my thoughts and feelings by pouring them into the metaphorical container of the image or images I'm working with.

Beginning the poem with a personifying question allowed me to skip over any world building that longer-form writing requires and established the rules of the poem's fantasy logic upfront. The opening line of this piece—*Why do cantaloupes wish to resemble the moon . . . ?*—lets the reader know right away that this is a world where cantaloupes have their own inner lives, longings, and anxieties.

Writing poems is always, ultimately, an inquiry into the self, and my poems are often disguised confessions, but by using the cantaloupes as my proxy, I reveal other images and ideas that would not have arisen were I writing from my own experiences. For example, the idea that the cantaloupes are *undone by human fingers*, while the moon is not, is a notion that only occurs to me as I consider my feelings within the imaginative confines of the cantaloupe and its reality. This is why personification is such a productive way to work; it is an act of collaboration between you and the object or image you are working with. What finally emerges on the page is neither wholly one's self nor wholly the object that is being personified; it is a marriage between the two, something that extends, ideally, to both the personal and the universal.

Sample Poems

The Pining Goldfish

Why would a goldfish wish to be a carrot?
This lucky fish in its dazzling suit
would make even Midas envious.
Finning in its round world, lush
java ferns drifting, flakes of food
falling like manna onto the surface of its universe.
Did its bowl get too small, too murky?
Did it get tired of being watched?
The carrot is left alone. It lives
below ground, folded in hard gritty dirt.
Its roots grow like an unkept scraggly beard.
It's a shade of orange that'll never shine.
It's fated to be yanked, chopped,
and whittled down. Maybe one day,
the carrot will fulfill its promise
of bringing good vision for someone.
Yet the goldfish is the star of carnivals,
a symbol of fortune. If lucky enough,
it can even find itself in a pond
surrounded by roots and flowers.

—Robin Rosen Chang

Blooms

Why do artichokes, glory-crowned with knife-sharp spikes,
glance heavy-hearted at the zinnia? When, after all, they are
fist-furled into a tight bouquet of dark green, charmed
with dusty armor? Why are they not content, marching
their sturdy leaves round & round—spiraling tighter & tighter
to the choke, its exquisite down-like softness, its pale gossamer
growth tinged with amethyst, its own heart a treasure?

Instead, they wish for fanciful monikers and zinnia's pigment
value, for the saturation of Zahara Double Fire, an orange-essence
spinning its petals like a parasol. Or Aztec Sun, a squat
pinecone-shaped zinnia, bursting fingers lemon-tipped,
dancing red to an orange-cushioned center, sprouting
straight-standing yellow stamen. A name gifted with joy-sparks,
Swizzle Scarlet swirls like a red & white barbershop pole,
proud of itself and its end-of-the-alphabet-flower name, zinnia.

Zinnia's Candy Land color blaze, its backbend stretch
to sun is showy—masking its weak spine, a soft stem
that droops under beauty weight, that gets tucked
in green plastic tubes for vased bouquets.
Artichokes stand solid—dark globes that prickle, that sport
sturdy stalks, that shield their truth. Once trimmed
of their spikes and gently steamed, artichokes bloom
to a shiny green, open shy hearts to humble hands. They allow
the gentle unfurling of protection to fall, allow tongue to move
and mouth to wrap around their softened leaves; allow lips
to pucker with lemon and butter, allow teeth to suck
leaf-treasure clean. Artichoke may be a lowly vegetable,
but it begins with the breath-sound of our alphabet;
it bears down with its quiet strength, then opens to reveal
the hush of its delicate perfection, its singular essence.

                    —Holiday Goldfarb

Bonus Prompts: Personification

—Kerrin McCadden

1. Who or What Are You?

Claim the identity of an object that metaphorically represents how you sometimes feel about yourself, e.g., a glacier, wrecked car, rocking chair, firework, tree stump. Begin or title your poem *The_____ (thing you are not)_____ (present tense verb/verb phrase),* then keep going. Begin the poem in an everyday activity. e.g., *The glacier sits down to dinner, The wrecked car collects books, The rocking chair dreams of stillness.* This can be a list poem, or maybe it will extend a single scene. So much the better if the poem is in the first person. It will probably end up being about you, anyway, but the forced comparison will likely send you toward complications and surprises.

2. Your Word Bank Comes Alive

Build a ten-word word bank according to this formula: a place name (a park, a neighborhood, a city, town, or country), an insect, a weather term/event, a tool, a geographical feature, a period or event in history, a term that has to do with furniture, and three words you like the sound of. Now, write a poem in the voice of an object you care deeply about. Let the object tell its story, or talk about you, make complaints, pontificate, or muse—but you must include all the words from your word bank. In a final draft, you might kick these words out of your poem, but their job is to push your imagination into sparking through the act of weighing what you love against words you might struggle to use.

3. What Are You Afraid Of?

Write a poem in the voice of something that terrifies you. This poem requires research. It must include: statistics, related historical events, superstition, a platitude, and scientific facts or hypotheses. Also, include a question and/or a retraction. Somewhere after the two-thirds mark, the speaker should address you in some way. It would be chilling to make this address direct—calling you by name, but it can also address the reader, or any *you*. Name the speaker in the title.

IX. Figurative Language: Hyperbole

If it's darkness we're having, let it be extravagant.

—Jane Kenyon

Craft Talk: Firing Fred and the Power of Hyperbole

—Peter E. Murphy

A million years ago I was a bartender at a trendy club in New York City. It had live music seven nights a week and lines that stretched around the block. The cramped dance floor overflowed with sweaty twenty-somethings who paid cranked-up prices for watered-down drinks. I was a budding poet who had written a series of bar poems. One, a parody, included the unfortunate line, *Willie Sutton at the cash register*. Willie "The Actor" Sutton was a Depression-era bank robber famed for using disguises such as a cop, a mailman, a Santa Claus, and, apocryphally, even a nun, in his heists.

While the other bartenders thought the poem was a gas, no one took it seriously except for the boss, who fired Fred, a new bartender he didn't like. *I knew that jerk was stealing from me*, he said. When I told him I'd made it up, that it wasn't true, he asked, *Why would you write it if it wasn't true?* This man, who could pick a winner at Aqueduct by glancing at a mare half a mile away, but who'd never read a poem in his life, taught me about the power of poetry, and especially about the power of hyperbole. Sorry, Fred.

I include the following requirement in every writing assignment I give: *Tell a secret, tell a lie, and never tell anyone which is which.* You're probably wondering why I would ask a person to tell a secret, which you would never tell. However, when sharing something private, writers make themselves vulnerable, thus creating a kind of intimacy with the reader. I urge writers to do this, and if it's too much, I suggest they write it anyway, then cross it out, and the residue of that intimacy remains.

Tell a lie—of course, I stole this from Kenneth Koch's 1970 classic, *Wishes, Lies, and Dreams: Teaching Children to Write Poetry*. When I ask writers to tell a lie, what I'm really asking them is to use their imagination. The easiest way to tap into this treasure chest is to exaggerate, to use hyperbole.

Kim Addonizio ponders the Freudian question *What do women want?* in a poem by the same name. Her diffident persona decides a red dress will improve her life and make her the woman she will never be. She describes the shops in her tawdry neighborhood as her desire builds momentum. She starts by saying she wants the dress flimsy and cheap. Then she says, *I want to walk like I'm the only woman on earth and I can have my pick.* She works herself into a verbal frenzy as she says, *When I find it, I'll pull that garment from its hanger like I'm choosing a body.* Addonizio's persona concludes her rave by saying,

> I'll wear it like bones, like skin,
> it'll be the goddamned
> dress they'll bury me in.

This is hyperbole at its best, rhyming, outrageous, and true.

In Tom Wayman's "Did I Miss Anything?" the speaker answers, in an unexpected way, this question frequently asked by students who miss class.

> Everything. A few minutes after we began last time
> a shaft of light descended and an angel
> or other heavenly being appeared
> and revealed to us what each woman or man must do
> to attain divine wisdom in this life and
> the hereafter.

Yikes! If I were his student, I'd make sure I never cut another class, but I'm not. I'm a poet, and I love his over-the-top response.

Hyperbole, by definition, is overblown, as in the examples laid out here. Like all high-powered weapons, it is best used in moderation, or it can nuke an entire population of poems. But can there be a quiet hyperbole, a subtle exaggeration that whispers rather than shouts? You don't want to always scream at your reader when a softer voice might make your words sing.

In Robert Hayden's "The Prisoners," the poet is invited to read at a jail. To say he's nervous would not be an exaggeration. After the *guillotine gates . . . closed massively* behind him, surely an overstatement, he writes this gorgeous sentence: *We were locked in with loss.* Hayden describes the window-barred, *drab Rec Hall*, where his audience of inmates awaits him. Then he composes this brilliant, restrained hyperbolic sentence, *Hands intimate with knife and pistol, / hands that had cruelly grasped and throttled / clasped ours in welcome.*

Hayden shares another secret: *And I read poems I hoped were true.* Isn't that what we all hope for? We share his relief, and his accomplishment, in the last line of the poem, *It's like you been there, brother, been there, / the scarred young lifer said.*

Poem and Prompt

A Rogue Dream

after Olivia Gatwood

I get ready for my first day as the new girl in high school
already knowing what not to wear. I dress perfectly
to stand out and disappear. I know how to put on
makeup, and I do it exactly right. My hair
looks awesome, of course! I step onto the bus,
pause by the driver, raise my arms like a superstar,
and meet the eyes of my adoring audience.
Three different beautiful girls punch
each other in the face to have me sit next to them.
I decline and the school's most lovely, artsy boy
slides over to make room. He knows his feelings
and only goes too far
when he honestly misunderstands. He's one of the safer ones.

I walk down the halls and no one makes fun of me.
I pass the section of lockers where her locker is, and
she is there, taking a book out of her backpack.
She'll go running this weekend, as usual, and won't
be followed. The man who won't be following
her has already followed half a dozen women
to rape and kill and leave in the woods. But she won't be
followed. She'll survive her fate this time, and come back

to school on Monday, avoid the mean girls in the bathroom.
She'll pick on the new girl, call her a virgin of all things.
She'll limp her way through math, cheat a bit in science,
do pretty good in history and English. She'll graduate,
and go to the state school on a track scholarship. She'll
have two girls and keep them safe. She'll almost forget

about this other ending: her in the woods near her house,
staring at the ground beneath her, wondering why.

—Melanie Figg

The dream is a convention in literature. It allows the writer to give free rein to the imagination and to revise reality. Figg's treatment of the dream motif is unusual in that while one dream is occurring a second one slips in and takes over the poem.

Stanza 1 is devoted to the launching dream. This dream is a reimagining of the speaker's first day at a new school. She details her popularity, but from the ironic tone of the descriptive details, we infer that in real life, the speaker was not popular. Note the touch of irony as she dresses *perfectly / to stand out and disappear*.

Note also the use of hyperbole as the speaker raises her arms *like a superstar* for her *adoring audience*. The hyperbole conveys what the speaker wishes her real life had been like. Hyperbole is a risky figure of speech; if overdone, it can become unintentionally humorous. But Figg uses a light touch with the figure and makes it effective. This stanza also lays the groundwork for the rest of the poem as the speaker sits next to a popular boy who is *one of the safer ones*.

Stanza 2 is sparked by stanza 1's reference to the boy on the bus as *one of the safer ones*. According to Figg herself, stanza 2's rogue dream is based in reality and pertains to the fact that when she was a teenager in Vermont, a serial killer murdered nine local women, two of whom she knew. In the poem the speaker resurrects a murdered girl who returns to school and does what popular girls do. Notice that the speaker subtly shifts from first to third person.

In stanza 3 the speaker projects a future for the murdered girl.

The closing two-line stanza returns to reality and, in a painful image of the girl *staring at the ground beneath her*, reminds us of what really happened to the murdered girl.

✎ ✎ ✎

For your own rogue dream poem, first recall an unpleasant event that happened years ago, to you or to someone else. Or invent one. Perhaps moving to a new town, going to sleepaway camp, starting your first job or a new job. This event is the subject of the first dream and will be covered in stanza 1. Using first person, narrate the event as if you are relating a dream. Bring it to life with descriptive details.

In your next stanza, bring in the rogue dream, the one that intrudes itself into the poem, seemingly arriving uncalled for. It should be touched off by something in stanza 1's dream and should be something unpleasant that happened to someone other than the speaker. Again, include descriptive details. Switch to third-person speaker as you describe what happened to someone else. The star of this stanza is someone other than your speaker. Project a future for the star of the rogue dream. Then swing back to reality at the end, reminding us of what really happened.

In subsequent drafts of your poem, hone your descriptive details, keeping the best ones and ruthlessly discarding the excess. Try to work in some irony, some hyperbole, and some contrast. Work on the switch from first- to third-person speaker, but feel free to discard it if it doesn't work.

Commentary: Hyperbole and the Dream Convention

—Melanie Figg

"A Rogue Dream" came from a prompt based on "I'm always trying to make my poems timeless," a poem by Olivia Gatwood in which she uses a playful voice and includes the phrase *rogue dream*. I had been writing poems for a new book—a hybrid memoir that includes material about the fact that when I was a teenager in Vermont, nine local girls and women were killed by a serial killer and I knew two of the victims. I loved the idea of writing a poem that went rogue on its content—reimagining my rough freshman year in high school, and creating a different ending for another girl, if only in a poem.

Teenagers are expert exaggerators—the eye roll!—and masters of hyperbole. I hated the high school I attended as a ninth grader—I was new and didn't fit in; I was targeted for bullying and simultaneously ignored. The very act of writing this poem using hyperbole freed me up—not only from my rutted narrative of myself as a teenager and my year at that school, but also from a writing rut of rarely writing a funny poem, or being playful while writing.

Maybe all dreams, daydreams and sleep-dreams, have elements of hyperbole. Dreams are exaggerations by nature—a friendly way our subconscious elbows us for attention—*see that? What the hell is that about?* In poems too we're able to throw ourselves into different futures, more glamorous situations, safer situations. So the idea of using the dream convention to talk about my high school experiences made sense, and also felt like a relief. Hyperbole gave me a kind of armor to revisit that period in my life, to change the narrative. It gave me a way to be playful about some memories that, up until then, were hard and very charged for me.

I often tell my students and writing clients that this is one of the real benefits of art: poems can become an alternative lens that can alter not only the reader's view of the world, but also our own view of the past and of ourselves.

Sample Poems

Hide-and-Seek

Northern Virginia, 2002

The week I teach poetry to fourth graders,
my students scramble up slides at recess

and blister their fingers on monkey bars.
They swipe the shoulders of each other's

striped t-shirts and erupt in a chorus
of *Not it! Not it!* They are not squirming

in desks, locked down because a sniper
is targeting strangers. A teen in search

of a father is not crouching in the trunk
of a blue Chevy Caprice, taking aim

at bus passengers and landscapers
and drivers pumping gas. On this day,

a 25-year-old woman vacuums Cheerios
from the back seat of her mini-van

at a Shell station and returns home
to her toddler daughter whose favorite

word is *why. Why dogs bark? Why
thunder go boom? Why babies cry? Why?*

Why? A liquor store clerk rings up
the last sale of the night and heads back

to his garden apartment where he falls
asleep to *Law & Order* reruns.

Their families will not have to ask *why*. I write
personification on the board. *What word*

is hiding inside? I ask. I'm looking, of course,
for *person*. In this version, there is only one boy

in the world hungry for attention, and he shoots
his arm in the air and answers *cat*.

—Erin Murphy
published in *One Art: A Journal of Poetry*

Natural Disaster

Splintered, scattered two-by-fours, window frames, wallboards,
a dresser with the drawers still closed. My brother's massive
tulip tree had flattened roof and bedrooms, hallway and study.
His house unscathed. His neighbor's house
destroyed. Storm-soaked souvenirs, photographs,
and shattered crystal await a crane to dislodge the beast.
My brother cannot shake his sense of guilt, produces
copies of arborist reports, receipts for pruning.

At night he cannot sleep, then finds himself stuck
in the dream where our parents did not divorce.
No one felt bereft of family. Mother took pride
in his interests, voiced no disappointment when
he did not go to med school. If sometimes
in his dream mother had a second husband,
that one did not drink, or shout or criticize.

Brother's neighbors seem so cheerful,
If not cheerful, then accepting. They repeat,
It's only things. No one got hurt. They'd been
tidying the kitchen, and fled from home
as the crown crashed down. Brother would prefer
them angry, would understand their blame.
The hollow beneath the trunk looks impossibly
shallow, the torn roots thin and insubstantial.

—Jessica de Koninck

Poem and Prompt

Love Poem without a Drop of Hyperbole

I love you like ladybugs love windowsills, love you
like sperm whales love squid. There's no depth

I wouldn't follow you through. I love you like
the pawns in chess love aristocratic horses.

I'll throw myself in front of a bishop or a queen
for you. Even a sentient castle. My love is crazy

like that. I like that sweet little hothouse mouth
you have. I like to kiss you with tongue, with gusto,

with socks still on. I love you like a vulture loves
the careless deer at the roadside. I want to get

all up in you. I love you like Isis loved Osiris,
but her devotion came up a few inches short.

I'd train my breath and learn to read sonar until
I retrieved every lost blood vessel of you. I swear

this love is ungodly, not an ounce of suffering in it.
Like salmon and its upstream itch, I'll dodge grizzlies

for you. Like hawks and skyscraper rooftops,
I'll keep coming back. Maddened. A little hopeless.

Embarrassingly in love. And that's why I'm on
the couch kissing pictures on my phone instead of

calling you in from the kitchen where you are
undoubtedly making dinner too spicy, but when

you hold the spoon to my lips and ask if it's ready
I'll say it is, always, but never, there is never enough.

—Traci Brimhall

Hyperbole is the language of love. Brimhall makes ample use of this figure in her ironically titled poem. Almost every line contains hyperbole; the poet indulges, goes overboard. Some of the hyperbolic declarations are expressed in similes: *I love you like the pawns in chess love aristocratic horses* and *I love you like a vulture loves / the careless deer at the roadside.*

Sometimes the poet gives us two similes together, e.g., *I love you like ladybugs love windowsills, love you / like sperm whales love squid.* Often the word *like* is used to make a simile but sometimes it's used as a verb: *I like that sweet little hothouse mouth / you have. I like to kiss you with tongue, with gusto, // with socks still on.* Brimhall indulges in lively verbal gymnastics.

Even some of the straight declarative sentences are hyperbolic in their excess: *I'll throw myself in front of a bishop or a queen / for you* and *I'd train my breath and learn to read sonar until / I retrieved every lost blood vessel of you.*

Note that the poet draws her hyperboles from diverse fields, e.g., mythology, marine biology, nature, the insect world, chess, the body, roadkill, and food.

The poet formats her poem into couplets, an ideal form for a poem about love between two people. Notice the use of enjambment. The spilling over of one line into the next line or the next couplet adds to the feeling of the speaker's exuberance and moves the poem forward at a good pace.

There's a syntactical shift in the fourth from the last couplet. Now the speaker tosses in a series of fragments: *Maddened. A little helpless. // Embarrassingly in love.* Then the final three couplets consist of one long sentence as the speaker expounds on her love.

Finally, note that Brimhall uses a direct address to *you*, her beloved. This gives the illusion of a private conversation taking place, one we are lucky enough to eavesdrop on.

✐ ✐ ✐

For your hyperbolic poem, first choose a subject. This could be your own beloved, real or imagined, but might instead be your child, your dog, a favorite food, maybe even yourself.

Brainstorm a list of hyperboles, some as similes, some as declarative sentences. Draw from a variety of fields. Be playful and extravagant.

Now begin your draft. Let your first-person speaker address the beloved as *you*. Incorporate the hyperboles.

As you revise, work on alternating similes and declarative sentences. Work in some fragments. Close your poem with one long sentence.

Format your poem. Couplets are beautiful and ideal for a love poem with one speaker and one auditor, but another format might work just as well.

Sample Poems

Love Poem with Old-Fashioned Extravagance

I love you like night-blooming jasmine loves the night,
the way a fisherman loves night crawlers. I dig

the way you dance, the way other women swoon
just watching you lead me around the room. We work

together like Fred and Ginger, like Wilma & Fred.
You're my *yabba dabba doo*. I love the way your hair

goes silver in sunlight, the way your day-old whiskers
ruin my neck. I hunger for you, thirst for you the way

my mom wanted her bourbon. I'd drink you neat.
I like it when you lean into me the way Andretti

used to lean into the curves. You can rev me up
with your slow hands. Come to me, *my knight*

in shining armor. I'll be Ethel Thayer to your Norman.
For you, I'd unbury my diary, read you back to love.

Faithful love. Undying love. Old bone-clattering, shake
the chandeliers in the dining room below us love.

Let's make out, embarrass our grandkids
with too much PDA. After all, YOLO.

I'm a lost cause, baby. My love isn't moonlight
on magnolias; I'm Atlanta, burning for you—

this is love that's risky, as familiar as a cat
loving her kitten by its neck, like quicksand

absorbing a body, like Spanish moss on live oaks,
like Saran Wrap on tomorrow's leftovers.

—Gail Comorat

February, Don't Let the Door Hit You on Your Way Out

I love that we've come to your final dreary, drab,
miserable day. Love that I can say, farewell bleak February,

love that you're over again for the year. I love
that I can count the ways I'm glad we're through with you.

There is no road I wouldn't go down to avoid
laying eyes on you again. The low road,

the high road, the yellow brick road, even
the road to nowhere. Your friends are few

and even none of them are crying,
and the rest of us? We're glad to see

you go. You're the eyesore, the plague,
the Eeyore of the calendar year

because you make us so darn SAD and blue,
withholding daylight the way you do.

You're as appetizing as a mound of
mushy lima beans in a pot of stew,

and what is it with that *r* before the *u*—
is it silent or not? Don't make us guess,

as that only triggers more distress. Your days
were numbered from the start and aside

from St. Valentine and silly candy hearts
you're quite honestly the month that's cursed,

like the poisoned apple in Snow White. Mirror,
mirror on the wall, who's the gloomiest month of all?

It's you, February. You're short on days
that bring a smile. Cheerless. You bring me down,

down to the pit of despair with no relief. White
on white, gray on gray, monotone day after day,

nothing but drab and drear. You're all
dismal skies with no relief.

You're a bad case of the weather woes
and ongoing grief. From one day to the next,

you're a muddled mess:
first snow, then ice, some rain, then sleet—

before you know it,
things turn to slush and muddy mush.

Face it, Feb, you're the month that sparks no joy
and as Marie Kondo would say, *Throw it away*.

So I'll be glad—backflips and handsprings glad—
to watch you dissolve and melt away.

                    —Kim Klugh

Bonus Prompts: Hyperbole

—BJ Ward

1. The Larger Than Large Absence

Freewrite about absences. Start with real, ordinary absences and grow bigger with each subsequent image, transitioning into the hyperbolic, ending with some kind of absence that feels larger than the other absences. Examples of such poems include Elizabeth Bishop's "One Art" and David Daniel's "Ornaments."

2. Mixing the Senses

Synaesthesia, a mixing of the senses, by its nature, can seem hyperbolic—a breaking down of the wall between senses. Examples include Robert Frost's "From what I've tasted of desire" or the "bald cry" in Sylvia Plath's "Morning Song." Write a twelve-line poem about something you recall relatively clearly from your teenage years. You must incorporate ten examples of Synaesthesia within these twelve lines.

3. Hyperbole Reversal

Write a love poem (romantic, filial, or any other type of love) in which you actively refute hyperbole. An example of this is William Shakespeare's Sonnet 130, "My mistress' eyes are nothing like the sun."

X. Figurative Language: Apostrophe

I saw the gooseflesh on my skin.
I did not know what made it. I was not cold.
Had a ghost passed over? No, it was the poetry.

—Sylvia Plath

Craft Talk: Apostrophe as Shortcut to Discovery

—Dion O'Reilly

In William Butler Yeats's poem "Among School Children," the elderly speaker inspects a classroom and gazes at the children. He remembers the unattainable lover from his youth and begins an eight-stanza meditation. In the final stanza, he experiences a lyrical moment of unity as he addresses an absent tree and a dancer:

> O chestnut tree, great rooted blossomer,
> Are you the leaf, the blossom or the bole?
> O body swayed to music, O brightening glance,
> How can we know the dancer from the dance?

Although definitions vary, in general, we can say these lines are apostrophe—a form of direct address to an absent entity, person, object, or concept. Imagine this stanza without the yearning *O* that often begins apostrophe—the *O* that resembles a wailing mouth. Imagine if there were no pair of *O*'s in the penultimate line, accelerating the pace of yearning. By directly addressing the absent beings, the closing revelation is tinged with loss, deepening the speaker's ambivalence and pathos. By directly questioning the absent figures, Yeats creates uncertainty and entreaty.

Indeed, without apostrophe, the lines would be something like the following: *The chestnut tree is a great rooted blossomer, composed of leaf, blossom, and bole. The dancer sways to music with a brightening glance. We cannot tell the dancer from the dance.* This is cold exposition. Furthermore, there is nothing to differentiate those lines from the rest of the poem, which is mainly contemplative. In other words, there is no turn. We do not experience amped up, complex emotion. The all-important discovery is weakened or non-existent.

So we can say—based on this canonical piece and contemporary poetry too—that the apostrophe is a handy piece of craft. It both creates a turn and turns up emotion. In Mathew Dickman's

"Fire," for example, the poem begins with a direct address to the fire in the form of a happy song: *Oh, fire, you burn me*, a friend sings under the stars as the group enjoys a campfire. Throughout the poem, Dickman explores the concept of fire, conflating it with the course of his life and his family's use of alcohol and drugs. The last lines of the poem are an upwelling, impassioned study of fire. The poem flares as the narrator directly addresses a series of inanimate objects:

> . . . oh, falling elevator—
> you keep me, oh, graveyard—
> you have been so patient, ticking away, smoldering—
> you grenade. Oh, fire,
> the first time I ever took a drink I was doused with gasoline,
> that little ember perking up inside me, flashing, beginning
>   to glow and climb.

Apostrophe not only intensifies emotion, it also zooms in like a microscope and clarifies. In Danusha Laméris's poem "The Moons of August," the speaker considers the many names for the moon. Mainly a list poem with a question, the poem turns when the speaker contemplates her losses. She cries out to a distant, unresponsive moon, and we experience an opening to pain. We feel her frustration and acceptance as she renames the satellite, thereby redefining and exploring her grief.

> . . . Oh Watcher, you
> who sees all that is born
> and all that dies
> tonight I name you
> Switchblade moon,
> Toss in the Towel Moon,
> Moon Turning to Sand,
> Empty Rice Bowl,
> Dust Moon, Salt Moon,
> Ash Moon,
> Blink of an Eye Moon.

One of the most powerful poems of the last few decades, Marie Howe's "What the Living Do" is entirely apostrophe. A kind of love letter to a deceased brother, the speaker shares quotidian moments of her life: *Johnny, the kitchen sink has been clogged for days, some utensil probably fell down there. / And the Drano won't work but smells dangerous, and the crusty dishes have piled up.* She ends the poem with something akin to a complimentary close: *I am living. I remember you.* It is hard to imagine this poem without the apostrophe. It would be a dry accounting, lacking the poignancy of speaking into the void of her beloved brother's absence.

Apostrophe falls nicely into a zone between exclamation, statement, dialogue, and—sometimes—the imperative or interrogative. In other words, a change in syntax that directly confronts the unknown, unseen, or unresponsive. Such changes delight the reader and mimic our internal dance between contemplation, memory, and dialogue. When we feel most hopeless, we shift to prayer, which is, in essence, a form of apostrophe.

Apostrophe hints at the subjunctive with its reference to non-existent objects, changing the mode of the poem. This form of direct address does not expect a response from its object; it is hypothetical and speculative, appealing to the human tendency to engage in magical thinking, our desire to animate the universe. With its history of invoking the muses or the gods, apostrophe moves toward the archetypal, dreamlike, or mythic. Indeed, you might say apostrophe moves the poem toward another world.

Reader, I married him, says Charlotte Brontë, and we too are changed, satisfied for the speaker, resonating with her emotional state. Apostrophe dials up emotion, creates unity between the present and the absent, the living and the dead, the narrator and the reader. Most importantly, by speaking directly to the invisible, apostrophe moves the poem toward its discovery.

Poem and Prompt

The End of the Pier

I walked to the end of the pier
and threw your name into the sea,
and when you flew back to me—
a silver fish—I devoured you,
cleaned you to the bone. I was through.
But then you came back again:
as sun on water. I reached for you,
skimmed my hands over the light of you.
And when the sky darkened,
again, I thought it was over, but then,
you became water. I closed my eyes
and lay on top of you, swallowed you,
let you swallow me too. And when
you carried my body back to shore—
as I trusted that you would do—
well, then, you became shore too,
and I knew, finally, I would never be through.

—Nicole Callihan

The meaning of this poem is appealingly elusive, but it hints at being a love poem, that is, a poem about the end of love and how love transforms us. The poet writes from the first-person point of view. Employing apostrophe, the speaker addresses a *you*. She goes through a series of efforts to rid herself of this unidentified *you*.

Using metonymy, the speaker first tosses not the lover but his name into the sea. It flies back to her transformed into a *silver fish*, one of several lovely images. After another attempt to rid herself of him, he returns as *sun on water*. Later he is transformed into *water*, then into *shore*. At this point, the speaker concedes that she will never be free of him. Thus, we end with an epiphany, a discovery.

Notice the poet's use of punctuation. She uses four dashes, a casual mark of punctuation, and a single colon, a more formal mark.

Notice also the poet's use of rhyme. There's end rhyme—*sea* and *me*, as well as *you, through, do,* and *too.* There's also internal rhyme with *you, threw, flew,* and *too.* There's also repetition of the rhyming phrases *but then* and *and when.* These rhymes and recurring phrases create music and unity. The phrases, especially, act as connectors.

✐ ✐ ✐

For your poem of transformation, first choose a setting, e.g., the top of a building, the back of a boat, center of a garden, side of a bridge.

Then using first-person point of view, address an unidentified *you* who is not present. From your location, toss away, kick out, haul away something associated with a beloved, e.g., a smile, face, memory, scent. Contrive a way for what's been tossed away to return in a new form. Repeat this action four times, each time with a new transformation.

Arrive at a moment of insight or epiphany.

Use end rhyme and internal rhyme. Capitalize on a single sound.

Use two connecting phrases. Extra points if they rhyme!

Try some dashes.

Sample Poems

To the Top of Hawk Mountain

On a hike to the summit,
I tossed your eyes to the light
and you came coasting back into sight—
a hawk—all feather and hollow bone.
I shot you down and deplumed you.
But you were resurrected in stone
along the mountain slope: schist,
gneiss, and quartz—hardnesses
you thought to lock me in.
But I hammered it all out,
pounded you down to dust,
discarded back to a wind
that scattered you over earth,
fertilizing the fruit of my table,
providing me days on days of return,
to keep what I still can't earn,
to remember what I still can't learn.

—Michael T. Young

At the Trailways Bus Depot

I stood at the Trailways depot
and flung your smile
(which always flipped my heart)
down under the next bus leaving town,
but you came back singing—
as a musical note that got stuck in my head—
so I wrote you into a bluesy farewell tune
and said goodbye, that's that, I'm done, the end.
But lo and behold you came whining back to me—
as a mosquito in my ear, and I wasn't about to let
you get under my skin again. So I squashed you flat.
And I thought that was that.
But didn't you turn up next as a bad penny
that keeps reappearing? I finally stuffed you
into my pocket then slipped you into
a vintage gumball machine I spied.
Goodbye again, I said. This is it.
Enjoy the ride! But then you had the gall
to come back as a cherry gumball
that I popped into my mouth and was glad to
chomp on and savor—
until my jaw began to ache, and all your flavor
disappeared. This time I was finally done.
One last chew and then into the street
I spit out the wad—
let someone else be stuck with you.

—Kim Klugh

Poem and Prompt

Ode to Tissue

O little sail, how quickly you become
a pocket's wad or rumpled cloud inside
the corner of a purse. You get one glance
across a runny playground nose, one daub
of graveyard tears and then we crush you up
as waste, our intimate embarrassment.
Perhaps there is some dignity at least
in being passed, pristine still, in your box
pastiched with tulips, to soften a blow:
I'll help you leave him. We can bury
her dog tags. You have six months or less.
Perhaps there is some puny majesty
with new couples, nervous, panting in the glow,
who pluck you for the aftermath of love.
My friend's son, who stays a boy who's trapped
inside the body of a man, who closes
his eyes every other morning when a hand
that is not his shaves stubble from his face,
knows enough to hide the evidence of night.
My friend doesn't mind you, tissue, balled
and tossed beneath a bed. Each weekend when
he crawls to clean, he finds you light as light,
still bright past damaging, like the body
of the baby wren a cat left on my stoop.
To spare my sons I mummied it in you.
In our darkened woods you matched the snow
and hid for me the bankruptcy of flight.

—Adam Tavel

An ode is a poem of praise, sometimes of lofty subjects, sometimes of mundane subjects. Tavel has chosen an ordinary object for his poem, but he treats it with reverence. He begins with apostrophe, using the exclamatory *O* and addressing the tissue as *you*, as if it could hear, were animate and present, and could respond.

The poem is structured around a list of the various functions a tissue serves, some funny, some poignant. The tissue is useful at funerals and in softening bad news, or, as the poet says with a touch of humor, *to soften a blow*. It is used by lovers to clean up after sex. It serves as a shroud for a dead bird.

Tavel has some lovely metaphors sprinkled throughout the poem. The tissue is addressed as *little sail*. It is a *rumpled cloud inside / the corner of a purse*. Towards the end of the poem, the verb *mummied* likens the tissue to a burial shroud.

We also find some nice similes. For example, the tissue is *light as light*, which capitalizes on more than one meaning of the word *light*. That simile is quickly followed by another in which the lightness of the tissue is *like the body / of the baby wren a cat left on my stoop*.

The poem also contains some delightful images. Who doesn't see the familiar box of tissues *pastiched with tulips*? Or the boy *trapped / inside the body of a man* being shaved by his father? Or the startling image that ends the poem: a wren killed by a cat, dropped on the stoop, then wrapped in a white tissue and left in the woods on top of white snow?

This is a lovely poem to read aloud. We hear the alliteration of *box, blow*, and *bury* at line ends. We hear the alliteration of *perhaps, passed, pristine*, and *pastiched* as they are placed in close proximity to each other. We also hear the rhymes of *night, light*, and *flight* at line ends and the internal rhyme with *bright*.

✐ ✐ ✐

For your ode, first select an ordinary object, e.g., a salt shaker, the remote control, a tube of chapstick, a lightbulb.

Now make a list of uses for your object. Choose the five or six best ones.

Brainstorm some metaphors for your object: *It is a* _____.

Brainstorm some similes for your object: *It is like* (or *as*)_____.

Begin your draft with apostrophe, a direct address to your inanimate subject.

As you proceed, work in the items from your list of the item's uses.

Weave in some metaphors and similes.

Use descriptive details to create several images. Save the best one for last.

As you revise, polish your language. Bring in some alliteration and some rhyme.

Sample Poems

In Praise of the Potato

Unbiased diplomats,
the real staff of life,
earth almonds,
you give off ephemeral perfumes
in five thousand languages
from A to V:
Almond
Chelina
Fianna
Nicola
Vivaldi.
Gigantic pearls of the soil,
thin-skinned, but not overly sensitive,
willingly pried out
by the lucky and unlucky alike,
your wealth lulls the world
in the universal language
of food,
assimilates differences
of race, geography,
stylishly comingles with all customs,
mountain to flat land,
playful gnocchi to spicy masala dosa.
Chameleon comfort,
chewable wine,
masquerading as legitimate vegetable:
Oven fry wedges resisting
teeth with zesty new skins;
chips that turn a solitary meal
into a party of one;
on-the-run French fries,
naughty, self-fulfilling;
celebration-of-summer potato salad
accompanied by cicadas;

pan fries, sedated by caramelized onion;
essential ingredient of immortal stews
that put spring on the back burner,
make winter worthwhile.
I would not want a life
without you.

    —Maren O. Mitchell

Ode to the Afternoon Moon

You float the azure sky like a golf ball
tossed by a bored god this ordinary
sunny day, no purpose but tides.
At night you shine like a streetlamp
without a pole. Oh yes, women
depend on you. How else
to measure blood and birth?

The sheriff's helicopter churns
below you and six crows blow
like black scarves in wind.
One crow appears to land on you
but slides sideways off your icy
white orb—a snowman's head
falling into an endless blue drift.

   —Denise Low

Poem and Prompt

To My Pacemaker

My device, my implant,
my ticker's ticker,
the way some people name
their GPS or other gizmos
I should come up with something
cute and personal to call you,

since after all it's your I.D.
I flash at airport security
or the ballpark gate
to keep those magic wands
from lingering too near
your subtle magnetism.

It's you my right hand rests on
as I pledge allegiance
to your unflagging signal,
yours the shock that sets
me straight, a bolt
from the vascular blue.

In time, I'm told,
I'll hardly think of you,
won't listen for your echo
in my pulse. You'll be
that strong, silent type,
torch I carry beneath the skin,

star power in my chest.
Each morning the mirror
gives you top billing,
your scar the crooked grin
of some matinee idol,
you hero, you heartthrob.

                    —James Scruton

In this poem of apostrophe, the speaker talks *to* his subject rather than *about* it. The subject/auditor is a pacemaker which has recently been added to the speaker's body. The poem begins with three terms for the pacemaker: *My device, my implant, / my ticker's ticker*. These sound almost like terms of endearment, but are quite literal.

The speaker then provides some accurate visual details about the pacemaker, e.g., that it must be protected from the security wands used in public places. The poet uses additional imagery to further illuminate his pacemaker. We visualize the speaker with his hand over his heart during the pledge of allegiance, and we see the crooked but grinning scar on his chest.

Scruton also employs metaphors to describe the device. It is metaphorically *a bolt from the vascular blue* and later the *torch I carry beneath the skin // star power in my chest*. In the closing stanza, the pacemaker becomes a *matinee idol*, a *hero*, and a *heartthrob*.

The poet ends his poem as he began it, that is, with a series of three descriptive terms.

The poem seems to amble along and the tone of address is casual, but notice that it is structured formally as five 6-line stanzas, making for a nice contrast between tone and form.

✐ ✐ ✐

For your poem of apostrophe, choose an artificial part of the body as your subject. You might choose a filling or a crown, a wig, contact lenses, a transplanted organ, an artificial limb, breast implants.

Make a list of descriptive details about the artificial part. You might want to do some research for this.

Generate some metaphors by asking yourself, *What is this part like?* or *What does it remind me of?* or *What does it look (or sound or smell or feel) like?*

Begin your draft as Scruton does with a series of three terms of endearment. Speak directly to the artificial part of the body, addressing it as *you*. Maintain that direct address as you proceed.

As you continue your draft, draw details from your list. Let images emerge.

Scatter in some metaphors.

Try to achieve a casual, almost affectionate tone throughout the poem. After all, this artificial part is performing an important service for the body.

As you revise, strive for a formal structure using an equal number of lines per stanza.

Finally, try beginning and ending with a series of three items. If that doesn't work for your poem, feel free to remove it.

Commentary: Apostrophe as Matchmaker

—James Scruton

Noodling around in a notebook, I'm not sure there's a poem underway until a few lines set a certain tone, establish some kind of rhythm, and somehow provide me an angle. This last feature is crucial for me. Call it point of view, perspective: An *approach* is what gets me going, as in "To My Pacemaker."

Here, I was intrigued by the paradox of this medical marvel, a thing so sophisticated and so intimate at once. An ode seemed too exalted. But once I addressed my pacemaker conversationally, the fun started; it would be less a song than a heart-to-heart talk. Pun fully intended. The opportunity for wordplay, for metaphorical possibilities, seemed to open up from the tone of that initial list: *device* and *implant* and *my ticker's ticker*.

Throughout the poem there's a balance struck between the scientific/medical (*magnetism, signal, pulse*) and the emotional (*magic, allegiance, grin*), a low-key Keatsian negative capability that accepts the contradiction. By simply talking (confessing?) to this small electronic contraption now part of me, by keeping the focus on its peculiarities—from therapeutic electrical charge to minor inconvenience when entering some venue—I could hold the poem's focus, let image and metaphor reveal the little gizmo's personality. As my wife archly says, it's a love poem to my pacemaker. Either that or a piece of fan mail to a star, a hero, my own heartthrob after all.

Sample Poems

To My Titanium

Valentine's Day when a slip on ice broke
not my heart but my tibial plateau,
you lifted me back on my feet. You
gave me back mobility without

the risk for corrosion or interfering
with my body's fluids. In screws,
wires, and rods, you are light

and strong, able and willing to vow
to bear my weight for the rest
of my lifetime. Best partner, you
are non-magnetic, under muscle,

won't set off metal detectors,
don't send me to a secret room
for closer airport exams. Lifesaver,

grief-reliever, youthifier, you bind
to cadaver bone paste, hold up
for my turns and rapid moves, let me
stride and strut and dance again. You

release me to sleep like a girl, legs
bent to create our marriage bed,
welcome space for a cat or a dog.

—Joan Mazza

To the Two Screws in My Left Hand

My hardware, my titanium,
my two tiny screws
brushed like white paint
across bone in the x-ray, you could easily be
those screws that come with picture hangers,

three to a bag and too many to count
leftover in a shoebox labeled "nails & screws,"
but since surgery you've held bone
to bone below my ring finger,
fourth metacarpal no longer mine,

belonging now to the three of us.
You won't set off metal detectors
or pull paper clips from my desk,
but you align my edges
as you disappear into new growth.

And though I worried that cold would settle
in your threads and in January, at 30 below,
radiate out in 2 mm cyclones of deep chill,
I felt nothing. Not the nothing of
annulment or ghosting, not forgetting,

just a quiet cohabitation of life partners
lost in work, in separate rooms, each barely aware
of the other until one coughs or calls out. Sometimes
the scar buckles and reminds me I'm not alone
in this body, but with you, grafted, still growing.

—Diane LeBlanc

Bonus Prompts: Apostrophe

—Patricia Clark

1. Talking to a Missing Person

Write a poem directly addressing a person who is not present. This could be a historical figure, a celebrity, a writer/artist who fascinates you, perhaps someone deceased, or maybe someone in your family from whom you're estranged. Imagine an encounter, such as a meal together. Then write a poem in which you express what you could not have said to the actual person. Enrich the poem with details.

2. Animating the Inanimate

Choose an object you deem useful or closely connected to your life somehow—a table, a tool, a pair of favorite socks. Write a poem addressing this object. Bring in details. Make this encounter come alive. What is your issue or trouble with the object? There's no need to immediately address the object—you might have a few lines, or a stanza, before you directly address the object. Experiment with where you address it.

3. Conversing with an Idea

Write a poem addressing an abstract quality such as innocence, sorrow, doubt, or envy. Have a conversation in your poem with this quality and flesh out a scene where the reader can see and hear and imagine the encounter. As you work through the prompt, be playful and think outside of the box you're normally in.

XI. Syntax

As I altered my syntax, I altered my intellect.

—W. B. Yeats

Craft Talk: The Elusive Art of the Line Break

—Marilyn L. Taylor

Have you noticed? The minute somebody finds out you're a poet, you're likely to hear what I call the famous TCR, or Totally Clueless Remark, that drives most of us straight up the wall. It goes something like this: *The trouble with reading a poem these days is that you can't even tell it's poetry.* Or: *Isn't reading today's poetry just like reading cut-up prose?*

Your proper response, first, is to refrain from wringing the person's neck. Then you might say, as calmly as you can, *Well, no*—and proceed to explain, as clearly and gently as possible, that the importance, the subtlety, and the potential power of the line and where it breaks, has an amazing effect on the entirety of a poem.

You might start out by quoting former U.S. poet laureate Charles Simic, who puts it this way: *For me,* he says, *the sense of the line is the most instinctive aspect of the entire process of writing [a poem] . . . I want the line to stop in such a way that its break, and the accompanying pause, may bring out the image and the resonance of the words to the fullest.*

The statement is simple, but it's one that poets everywhere should seriously think about committing to memory, and then quoting whenever someone utters a TCR. And, of course, we should keep it firmly in mind every time we sit down to write a new free verse poem. And speaking of free verse, please remember that in poetry as well as in politics, freedom always needs to be handled wisely. Breaking up a line arbitrarily will get a poet nowhere; certain linguistic conventions will always remain. Although no rule states that you have to follow those basic conventions—there are no poetry cops out there—you should probably have good reasons for deciding not to. Keeping that caveat in mind, here are a few suggestions to consider— with the understanding that you can ignore them if you're after certain special effects:

1. Avoid end-stopping every line. An end-stopped line is one that consists of a complete grammatical unit—often a whole sentence, or a clause ending with a comma, semicolon, or period—with no enjambment, or spillover, to the next line. Too many of these in a single poem can lead to a very choppy read.

2. Try to avoid breaking up prepositional phrases, especially short ones. They're usually—*usually*, not always—much smoother and more readable when they're presented as one happy grammatical family, all on the same line.

3. Avoid breaking a line immediately following an article, like *a* or *the*. Unless the poem is long and skinny and in a terrible hurry, it's a move that almost always comes across as awkward.

4. If you can, end most of your lines with a strong word. Try for one that will nudge the reader down to the line that follows. Keep in mind that words like *that* or *whether* or *went* simply don't carry the semantic horsepower of words like *kneecap*, *frenzy*, or *pelican*. Why bury all that lexical energy in the middle of a line?

5. Resist the temptation to center the poem on the page. No matter how cute it might look, how much it might resemble a Christmas tree or a football or a caterpillar, a centered poem is usually a bad idea. Unless you've consciously set out to write a concrete poem in which the shape is part-and-parcel of the meaning, you're far better off leaving the text left-justified, or with very simple indentations.

6. On the other hand, don't always feel chained to the left-hand margin. Indentations can sometimes add rhythmic variety and provide a poem with an interesting, more sprightly look on the page. Do this with restraint, though. Haphazard arrangements might only serve to confuse, and/or drive an editor stark raving mad.

7. Try very, very hard to avoid ending lines with ellipses, especially at the end of a poem. Ellipses can cause a reader to think that those little dots are there because the poet just couldn't think of the right . . .

8. Finally, know that you can work miracles with Strategic Syntax. Syntax—also known as *word order*—is our ironclad English-speakers' agreement to structure our words into phrases and clauses in ways that can be understood by others. It's why, when someone bangs on the ceiling, we don't yell, *Hey, off it knock!* and why we'd say *Jack changed a tire* instead of *a tire changed Jack*—unless Jack has recently experienced an automotive epiphany. Simple, right? Sorry, no. Not for poets, anyway—because poets work in an environment where syntax often has less to do with grammatical rules than with subtle, artful special effects. For instance, couldn't T. S. Eliot have suggested, *Let's you and I go there* instead of *Let us go there, you and I?* And why did Robert Frost write *Whose woods these are I think I know* instead of the more instinctive *I think I know whose woods these are?* Are there actual discernable differences here? Definitely. And we sense them because of the poets' artful *manipulation of syntax*, which replaces mere efficiency and clarity with *significance*. You might even think of them as *assembly lines* of words, ready to arrange and rearrange until you've turned your next poem into a nuanced gift for your readers.

Poem and Prompt

Abandoned Shacks in North Carolina

Tucked beside the freeway, behind wings
    of barbed wire and stockless fields,

  they shoulder into dusk and fade.

Spigots frozen. Stone-hard hills.
    Sometimes, I want to disappear

  that simply—growing into dim pastures

with deer ticks and snakeskins,
    wing beats above.

  I want to be filled with wind

and winter's slow thaw, a hibernating light.
    Collapsing inside themselves

  they're almost beautiful, glittering

like forgotten temples out in the snow,
    cross-beams broken, doors unlatched.

  Like a bright hoof, the moon

stamps down through their missing slats
    and at last the night surrounds.

  Every star is sown; every field is blue.

—Rob Shapiro

The title of the poem identifies the topic and the setting, neither of which is mentioned within the poem. That's a good functional use of a title.

Notice the syntax of the poem. The first three lines comprise one sentence. Modifying phrases precede the subject (*they*) and the verb (*shoulder*). Stanza 3 consists of two fragments. That stanza ends with a sentence that begins with a one-word modifier followed by a declarative sentence: *I want to disappear* . . . The subject/verb combination is repeated in stanza 6, emphasizing the speaker's identification with the scene. Notice especially the beauty of the syntax in the sentence that begins in the second line of stanza 7 and concludes at the end of stanza 9: *Collapsing inside themselves // they're almost beautiful, glittering // like forgotten temples out in the snow, / cross-beams broken, doors unlatched.*

Another virtue of this poem is its imagery. Shapiro gives us images of the *freeway, wings of barbed wire, stockless fields, Spigots frozen,* and *Stone-hard hills.* With such images as these, the poet allows us to see the abandoned shacks and to feel the sense of isolation. The final line of the poem offers us two images in parallel structure, a perfect syntactical close to the poem: *Every star is sown; every field is blue.*

Finally, notice the visual beauty of the form of the poem. Shapiro alternates 2-line stanzas with 1-line stanzas. The second line of each 2-line stanza is indented. Each 1-line stanza is also indented but not as much as the second line of the 2-line stanzas.

✐ ✐ ✐

For your own poem, first select a scene of decay or destruction, e.g., a house or a building after a fire, an old pickup truck abandoned in a field, a heap of trash dumped in the woods.

Use your topic and setting as your title.

Freewrite a generous and detailed description of the scene. Do not mention the topic or setting except in the title.

As you move to your next draft, work on syntax. Alternate a variety of complex sentence structures with simple declarative ones and some fragments.

Polish your images. Keep them simple and specific.

Work on your format. You might imitate Shapiro's or invent your own form.

Sample Poems

Rahway, New Jersey: The Old House

The house my grandfather built
is a cinderblock bag of cracked ceilings

    and long windows.

Smaller than memory believes, this is
the front porch place of my childhood—

    old furniture fortress of windy nights

in an attic bedroom where closet curtains
kept me awake because they moved. This is

    the family house where my mother

came into the world and left it, where four
generations of family members spent their lives.

    Tonight, a broken window blinks back

the moon. Leaves move in the star-driven
dark, and the sound echoes lightly

    as if someone is whispering my name.

      —Adele Kenny

In Greenland, Glaciers Fall

Like sentinels falling fast
at the gates of the Queen's summer palace,

    they, too, go down, one by one,

predicting Nature's and our fates,
once-fixed futures, they'll come too late.

    Shallow they are not.

But undercut, they break apart,
these massive sheets of glistering white,

    they signal retreat and we in flight.

Depth is the culprit hastening shrinkage,
meltwater and the salty layer

    drivers both of change and loss.

We measure warmth and the salinity,
quantify the calving and new fracturing,

conclude our lack of means to stop
makes faster flow and level rise,

    philosophers to think; the scientists, surmise.

        No slow surrender, they to land.
        No adaptation, for us no plan.

        —Maureen Doallas

Poem and Prompt

Farmers' Market

It's Saturday, and the farmers' market
is in full swing, all of us drifting
heavy-bodied and happy,
like figures out of Breughel,
among the fragrant stalls of strawberries
and apples and red peppers, honey
in amber jars, Amish cheese,
great brown loaves of bread,
the world proffering its bounty.

And then he comes gliding among us
on his tiny electric wheelchair, barely more
than a rolling pedestal since there's not much
to move, just a head and torso, the little of him
Iraq gave back. He's wearing a Grateful
Dead t-shirt which the girl walking with him
must have pulled over his head
and fitted tenderly over his stumps
before the two of them went out
to the market on this fall morning,

the rest of us suddenly staring hard
at the radishes and green sheaves of corn,
for we have never seen such vibrant carrots,
nor radishes quite so brazenly red,
nor come so close to understanding
the potatoes, wakened from their deep dream,
drowning in the world's light.

—George Bilgere

Bilgere begins his poem with a setting: a local farmers' market on a Saturday. He describes the scene with just enough details to make it feel warm and inviting—people milling about among the fruits and vegetables, cheese, loaves of bread, and honey. We see colors and smell fragrances. Then into this scene, in the second stanza, comes an Iraqi War vet who's returned home missing all four limbs. He's so damaged that the shoppers turn their heads away.

Notice the touch of irony in stanza 2. The vet is wearing a *Grateful / Dead t-shirt*. That's a significant line break, making *Grateful* ironic and *Dead* a punch to the gut. This telling detail lets us know that this vet was once someone who loved music, who attended concerts. Notice too the touch of tenderness here as the speaker imagines the vet's female companion pulling the shirt *over his head* and fitting it *tenderly over his stumps*.

Stanza 3 returns to *the rest of us* who have turned away and are now staring at the fruits and vegetables which ironically have become more beautiful than when first mentioned. Their colors are more intense, the potatoes are more alive, in fact, personified as having awakened from their *deep dream*. While this is the same scene as in stanza 1, the emotional tenor of it is completely different because of what happened in stanza 2. Bilgere so deftly handles the simplicity of his scene that we see it and feel it.

Notice the poet's use of sentences. The first stanza is one nine-line sentence. Stanza 2 ends a sentence midway through line 5. The third and final sentence goes through the rest of stanza 2 and continues through stanza 3 for a total of thirteen lines. This use of the sentence and the line gives the poem unity and cohesiveness. It pulls us along.

✑ ✑ ✑

For your poem, choose a setting that's upbeat, that feels happy, e.g., the boardwalk, the circus or zoo, a local park, an ice cream parlor. Begin by describing a limited aspect of the setting. Get in some images and let them do some work. They should be carefully chosen and limited.

Now bring something into the scene that is difficult to witness, e.g., a person with a physical deformity, a parent being cruel to a child or a pet, a homeless person. Add a touch of tenderness to this part of the scene.

In stanza 3, return to the first part of the scene. Let the speaker describe it in a way that makes it different emotionally. Again, let your images do some work.

As you revise, see if you can follow Bilgere's same sentence structure: one sentence in stanza 1, one and a half in stanza 2, the half sentence from stanza 2 completed in stanza 3.

The three-stanza structure may work well for your poem, but if it doesn't feel right, try a different format. Try the three-sentence pattern, but, again, if it doesn't feel right, alter it during revision.

Sample Poems

At the Theatre

It's five minutes to curtain and the theatre
is like a summer night filled with crickets
and frog song, greetings and calls of recognition
pitched across rows of velveteen seats,
laughs flickering, the air vibrating
with the warmth of anticipated pleasure
together in this place of plush red,
brass railings and silken tassels, muses
and cherubim looking on from above.

And just before the lights go down
one more couple slides in apologetically
to their seats in front of me, and pile their coats
into the space between them so that they
lean slightly away from each other.
Their eyes meet once and their looks
are of such disgust and sadness
that I think the darkness that drops just then
is because of them and will never end,

but it does as the curtain opens, and I retrain
my mind back to the other people, everyone's
shoulders whisper-touching, aisle to aisle
linked humans, and all at once a laugh
at something onstage lifts from them in unison,
a wave upward, golden and hovering
like a firework before dispersing, its sparks
dripping back onto all of us, even onto the couple
in front of me, their stiff and lonely shoulders.

—Lisken Van Pelt Dus

Butterfly Exhibit

Thursday night and the butterfly exhibit
is crowded, people passing through
the air lock to keep non-native
butterflies from escaping, warm air
of the tropical exhibit giving faces
a rosy look, children already exclaiming,
Look, it landed on my hand!
A mossy scent glides on the air,
mist puffing out from sensors, a waterfall
splashing. There's a faint
sweet smell: orchids, lilies.

An old woman with bent back pushes
her walker, bumping over cobblestones,
face red, scowling with effort. When
the young man (her son?) tries to help,
she pushes his arm away, *I can
do it!* Tired, she takes her ease
on the walker's seat where now
a red admiral butterfly circles, flitting
like an angel, landing on her sleeve,
Oh, it likes me! Some of us
grab our phones for photos, selfies,

studying the banana plant growing ten
feet toward the high glass ceiling,
leaving the two of them alone near
the pond where at the edge fresh-cut
oranges offer nectar to the butterflies,
some looking a bit tattered, wing-torn,
it's been days since they emerged, nothing
escaping gravity's wear and tear, a few
bumps and falls, grace found in moon-
light filtering down, such as it is.

—Patricia Clark

Poem and Prompt

Senior Cut Day

An act of defiance: I decided to show up,
attend every class, even take notes
though you couldn't do much with three or four students,
either Brian Hoffer with his coded binder
and early-admissions letter to Brown,
or Megan Dennis, recluse cellist, one absence shy
of being held back. While my friends played hooky,
drove to Jones Beach with Frisbees
and six-packs, expired sunblock
and disposable cameras, I stayed and ate lunch
with sophomores, let them in on my own private joke.
It was 1999. The Rapture at hand.
Our President was talking blowjobs
on C-SPAN. Getting high that night
in the bowling-alley parking lot, I heard Andre
pantsed Erin, how Goth Jimmy stripped
to swim, so pale he blinded the beach.
Marilyn Manson seared our ears, our '86 Mazdas
and rusted Fords. I could feel him slither
through caked makeup. I could hear
spring skidding towards summer,
that deep heat we worshipped and feared.
Who knew where any of us would be in a year?
Pot smoke rose and clouded our windows. I chose
a college whose mascot was extinct.

—Jared Harél

Harél begins with a special day in high school, one most of us
remember. But while the speaker recalls this day, what he best
remembers is going against the current; instead of cutting school
that day, he decided to show up and attend all classes.

The poet captures the atmosphere of the time by providing concrete details. He includes the names of a few other students who were in school that day. He tells us the year was 1999, the Rapture was at hand, and Clinton was misbehaving in the White House. Later, he mentions the music of the time and the cars.

In the last part of the poem, we learn what the students who cut school did on their day. Then three lines from the end, the poet stops us with an abrupt question, one that forces us to contemplate the future.

Notice Harél's mastery of complex sentence structures. The first sentence goes on for seven lines, the next for 5 lines. Then we get two very short sentences, one of them a fragment: *It was 1999. The Rapture at hand.* The pace slows down. We stop and pay attention. Soon the poet returns to long sentences, then the question, then a few short sentences.

✎ ✎ ✎

For your poem, first choose a special day back in high school when you went against the current. Maybe the prom you didn't go to, the graduation you skipped, the Honor Society ceremony you chose not to be part of. What did you do instead?

Feel free to choose a day that wasn't part of high school, but keep it in the past. Perhaps your wedding which at the last minute you decided not to show up for, or maybe the jury duty you skipped out on, a family reunion you decided was not for you, or the funeral you didn't attend. What did you do instead?

Make a list of some specific details pertaining to the event. What year, day, or time was it? What was the popular music then? What was a top news story? What were the popular cars?

Now begin your draft using the above material.

When you are well along the way and feeling like your poem is winding down, insert a forward-looking question.

As you revise, try to achieve the syntax that Harél employs. Get in some long, complicated sentences that contain lists and a series of phrases. Vary the pace with some short sentences. Use a fragment or two.

Commentary: The Music in the Syntax

—Jared Harél

"Senior Cut Day" is anchored in an *act of defiance* that felt, even in the moment, both utterly pointless and critically important. Like many high schoolers, I wanted to be myself, but didn't quite know who that person was. In composing this poem, I aimed to honor those twin impulses of conviction and uncertainty, while utilizing rhythm and syntax to achieve what Stephen Dunn calls *artful talk*.

Looking back, I notice my first-person speaker opens with a kind of casual boast that unravels as the poem moves down the page. Longer sentences grab at late-90's particulars—coded binders and disposable cameras—while shorter ones work to punctuate and emphasize. Because I'm a drummer as well as a writer, I arrived at these sentence structures by reading early drafts out loud, time and again, often tapping my foot along until tone and tempo clicked into place. I guess you could say the overall effect was deliberate to the extent that, like so many aspects of craft, syntactical variation works best when absorbed, then put out of one's mind.

The final third of the poem utilizes the five senses and a series of *er* slant rhymes—*slither, hear, summer, feared, year*—to build an anxious momentum. The poem's sole question, posed two lines before the end of the poem, underscores the speaker's growing doubts about himself, his friends, and their collective *clouded* future.

Sample Poems

High School Dance

Surprising no one, I skipped the ninth-grade dance.
I didn't have a flattering dress, shoes to match,
styled and conditioned hair. Cecelia surely went
popping into the girls' bathroom to roll her skirt shorter
like her sister taught her. Irene slathered on make-up
thick as a middle-aged realtor. The music was too loud;
fast dances made them giddy; slow dances even more.
Those slow dances, who danced with who, and where
their hands were, would be dissected over lean lunches
for days. My friends and I hung out in the park
across from City Hall, behind a hedge concealing us
from passersby but revealing a view of the clock tower.
We smoked dope and drank dry Chilean wine Chris snuck
out of the house. Marie and Chris might have been
broken up that night, or full on making out; Lori and Matt
giggled and exchanged smoke pretending they weren't
kissing. Patty and I had boobs but not boys
so we climbed a tree, sat in the crook of a low branch
peeling bark and watching the moon rise.
It was spring 1973. Watergate was more than
a hotel but the hearings were not yet televised.
Nixon was still in office presiding over the
Vietnamization of Vietnam. We marched
in used jeans from Goodwill, flowers embroidered
on back pockets. We debated who Carly Simon thought
was so vain. Some of us are lawyers now, life coaches,
librarians. Brokers to the arts. We are not the people
our parents warned us about. Were the answers ever
blowing in the wind?

—Elizabeth S. Wolf

College Senior: Vocational Blues

What grain is it, in life, we go against—
as though it were yards of fabric or a piece
of meat? I wanted to defy my mother and three
sisters before me: I would graduate, and no,
I wouldn't be a Mrs. with a ring. My boy-
friend then said a degree hardly mattered. "Guess
I'll get mine first and then decide," I said.
It was the 60s—Nixon in the White House, hands up
in vees—*I'm not a crook!* It was all protest
and discontent, my friends Paul and Tom escaping
Vietnam by lucky dates, the silent majority called out
to speak up, and refusing, per usual. I didn't walk
in a ceremony but the campus, the place, I held
sacred, especially the library and historic quad, pink
in springtime with cherry trees. I spun blood
samples in the U Hospital for work, trudging home
late or pedaling my ten-speed. In memory, always,
Drumheller Fountain aligned precisely with Mt. Rainier.
Who knew what would happen to any of us?
Some years before, a mob tore off campus, breaking
windows, burning buildings on the Ave over several
nights. What future could rioters see? That's where
my '65 Plymouth Valiant sat, on 15th street, that I
dreamed about before leaving for good: the word *aim*
written large by my finger in window fog.

—Patricia Clark

Bonus Prompts: Syntax

—Jennifer Franklin

1. The Negative Confession Poem

Write a first-person confession poem in the negative. Choose an event that was dangerous or unwanted. In your poem deny or negate what happened. This syntactical device can be a successful way of underscoring and emphasizing traumatic events. It is also a great way of creating tension. Begin the poem with a rejection of what the speaker experienced, e.g., *He did not lock me in the room when I returned home an hour late.* Continue in that manner.

2. Using Syntax to Make an Object Special

Think about an object that has deep value to you that would not be evident to an outsider, e.g., a photo, a ring, a vintage hat, or an old baseball mitt. Write a poem about this special object without being sentimental. Focus on unusual language. Give the poem jarring line breaks that keep the readers on their toes. Make us look at a familiar object in a new way. Make sure you vary syntax so your sentences are not all written in the same order with subject-verb-object. Make us form an attachment to the item through your lexical play and surprising turns of phrase.

3. Different Ways of Saying the Same Thing

Choose a favorite one-sentence quote from literature and build a poem around this quote. Let the line determine the subject of your poem. Intersperse the sentence at least three times throughout the poem and make sure you vary the syntax each time. Allow the repetition to assist in a debate and a dialogue so the reader understands the tension and conflict inherent in the struggle. For example, you might begin with a quoted line such as *It would be better if we parted.* That might later become *If we parted, it might be better,* and then *Would it be better if we parted?* The poem might end with *We could still part; it might be better.*

XII. Sonnet

There is often as much poetry between the lines of a poem as in those lines.

—Alexandre Vinet

Craft Talk: Bead on a String

—Diane Seuss

A lethal impediment to a writer's continued evolution is self-imitation. I think of certain musicians who make a fortune singing of poverty and who continue to sing of poverty long after they got rich singing of poverty. It is a difficult balance, holding to what is essential to your nature while challenging yourself to make it new. How does one build a body of work over a lifetime without writing the same poem over and over again? I have some thoughts, based on what has sometimes worked for me. I say *sometimes* because nothing is guaranteed. A writing life is hopefully long, and it is not particularly comfortable unless you sit yourself into the cozy chair of a particular style, tone, approach, form, and relationship to your subject and your reader, and stay there. But we don't want to sit in that chair, do we? We want to suffer for our art. Here's how I recommend optimal suffering for optimal benefit.

Take it in through the senses: To *have* seen/tasted/smelled/touched is not enough. One must ignite the senses daily, experience the *out there* with freshness, specificity, and—the hard part—with a degree of objectivity. Experience what? Whatever is in your vicinity. There is the panoply of natural things, arriving, waning, retreating. There is the human-made. Bicycles, buildings, Botticelli. The danger is in naming any of it beautiful (or ugly). Details, inhaled dispassionately, stock your image pond. Images, over time, gain the capacity to vibrate, levitate into metaphor. Metaphor, now and then, if we're lucky, extends its feelers into archetype.

Life is but a dream: Pay special attention to dreams, portents, psychics, tarot cards, and strange animals that show up in your vicinity. For instance, I woke with a start from a dream of sorts with the words *still life* emblazoned on the inside of my forehead. I love visual art, but I had no particular connection to still life painting. Still, I took the hint and did some research, which turned into the conceptual frame of my book *Still Life with Two Dead Peacocks and a Girl*. I was born into a town with a two-headed lamb as a mascot, so I've always been open to this sort of thing. If you're not, if you're one of those rationalists, just treat the gifts from the other side as randomness exercises. No telling where they will lead you, but you can be certain they will offer you a pathway out of the habitual.

De-situate yourself: Upend your setting. Go elsewhere for a while. I realize this is an economic issue, a class issue, a safety issue. I've attended residencies that were free of charge, if one were accepted, and this allowed me to explore a jarring, defamiliarizing landscape. Inevitably, I would spend the first couple of days in a state of terrible homesickness, which in earlier times was seen as a potentially deadly condition. The antidote for me seemed to be taking in the new landscape through my senses, allowing myself to experience the instability, and then—get to work. One residency was situated on an island overrun with rabbits. Rabbits in all their guises—researched, dreamed—became central to the work I was then generating.

We can also move our bodies into less familiar local landscapes. More importantly, we can de-situate our self-concepts. If you tend to be the hero of your poems, consider self-critique. If you tend to be right, dare to be wrong. If you lecture the reader, lecture yourself. If you're hard, try soft. If your diction *talks*, sing. Do a *fearless moral inventory* of yourself. If you have the privilege to stay above the fray politically, dive in. If you seduce, rob yourself of the masks seduction requires. Strip yourself of everything you think you are. *Then* write the poem. Life will eventually do this for you, of course. It will send in the elegant robber, just in the nick of time. As a wise woman once told me: experience the robbery, then find a way to love the robber.

Do a formal shake-up: If you've not done so, work in a given form for a while. There is really no way to self-imitate if you're reaching for end words in a sestina or writing toward lines from a borrowed quatrain in a glosa or compressing your great big Self into fourteen little ole lines in a sonnet. *Bring the balloon of the mind / That bellies and drags in the wind / Into its narrow shed*, Yeats advises. And he should know.

Given forms, even self-invented forms, are sure to corset you in ways that require creative problem solving. In my book, *Still Life with Two Dead Peacocks and a Girl*, I invented a sonnet composed of what Allen Ginsberg called American Sentences— basically a haiku without line breaks. My sonnet is fourteen lines, no rhyme or meter, but each line is seventeen syllables. And each sonnet, in this sequence, is ekphrastic, based on a still life painting. If all that weren't problematic enough, the sonnets are all placed in my rural, working class hometown. All these *givens* kept my analytical mind busy, which turned out to grease the hinges of a door that opened to the archetypes that reside hidden in the darker folds of my brain.

And if you're a devoted formalist? Enter the toothed wilderness of free verse.

Poem and Prompt

When in disgrace with fortune and men's eyes

I scroll through Facebook feeling sorry for
myself and pray to the absentee sky
daddy I don't believe in anymore
to free me from the green, eddying eye
of envy while I *like* the gorgeous selfie
of a woman in her 60s who looks
30, *wow!* a friend who won a poetry
contest I entered and lost, then *heart* the books
others have published, blank as a shadow
of who I could have been—but then you bring
the crossword and a steaming cup o' Joe
as warblers, cardinals, and kinglets sing
their golden oldies with the meadowlarks,
and white-faced Kasey, singing backup, barks.

—Beth Copeland

Copeland gets her poem underway with a borrowed line, this
one from Shakespeare's Sonnet 29. (This, by the way, is a great
way to get yourself writing on a day when you think you have
nothing to say.) She uses the line as her title and lets it run right
into the poem. The poem that follows is a Shakespearean sonnet—
fourteen lines consisting of three quatrains and a couplet. The
poem is written in iambic pentameter with a rhyme scheme of
abab cdcd efef gg. Typical of a sonnet, the poem has a *volta*, or
turn, this one occurring in line 10 and signaled by the word *but*.

Notice that the poem consists of one sentence.

While the poem hearkens back to earlier times, Copeland engages
a contemporary vocabulary drawn from the world of social
media. Her speaker, in a downcast mood, goes on Facebook—

she *scrolls,* she *likes,* she admires a *selfie,* and she *hearts* some books—all references to social media. The speaker provides enough details for us to infer that she suffers from envy of those more successful than she. Shakespeare's speaker was similarly afflicted.

Just as Shakespeare's young man was consoled by his beloved, so too is Copeland's auditor who arrives in the nick of time with coffee. The poem ends on a note of humor as the speaker's dog serenades her.

✎ ✎ ✎

To begin your own one-sentence sonnet, first find a line from another work.

Select a contemporary source for references, e.g., social media such as Twitter or Instagram, a TV show, computer technology, video gaming, physical fitness. Make a list of words from your chosen field.

Begin your draft using your borrowed line as your title or first line. If the line is famous and easily recognizable, no attribution is needed. If it's not famous, then play it safe and provide an attribution. Pick up from the title or first line and keep going. Each line must be at least three words.

Work the diction from your contemporary source into your draft.

Be sure to include a volta. A volta often begins with a word such as *but, then, however, although, though, still, yet.*

Try to employ the Shakespearean pattern of iambic pentameter and the rhyme scheme of *abab cdcd efef, gg.* But your sonnet may take whatever form you like. If you're confounded by the pattern, you may elect to exclude rhyme and/or meter.

As you revise, feel free to move or remove and replace your borrowed line.

Commentary: Fusing Old and New in the Sonnet

—Beth Copeland

I wrote "When, in disgrace with fortune and men's eyes" after poet Michael T. Young invited me to submit a one-sentence sonnet for a special issue of *Shrew* that he was editing. Since I'd never written a one-sentence sonnet before, I looked for examples and found Shakespeare's Sonnet 29. I used Shakespeare's first line as my title to signal the reader that Sonnet 29 is a springboard for my poem. Shakespeare addresses alienation, envy, and despair in his sonnet, so I listed occasions when I feel sorry for myself or envy the success of others on social media, something that hadn't existed in Shakespeare's day.

The volta, or turning point, of Shakespeare's sonnet takes place when the speaker thinks about his beloved and is reminded that he is fortunate. The volta in my sonnet occurs when I step away from Facebook to drink coffee, work a crossword puzzle, and listen to birds singing and my dog barking.

The original version I submitted to Michael T. Young had problems with meter. Fortunately, Michael suggested revisions that would make my sonnet stronger. The first four lines were fine, but the meter broke down in line 5. Michael suggested revising my original line—*of envy—I* like *the gorgeous selfie*—by deleting the em dash and adding *while* to make the meter more regular. Other minor changes were made to lines 7 and 8. The meter in the last four lines of my original sonnet was still irregular:

> coffee and the crossword, so I follow
> to the front porch where we rock on the swing
> as a glee club of warblers and skylarks
> greets us and our dog, singing backup, barks.

Michael pointed out that the stumbling meter might work if the content of the lines reflected disharmony, but since the subject is the singing of warblers and skylarks, the irregular meter was especially jarring. I revised the last four lines to restore the pattern of iambic pentameter.

Never underestimate the advice of an editor! Without Michael's guidance, my sonnet would be stumbling instead of published.

Sample Poems

"My Heart Flapped Like a Rag in My Ears"

Father, did your heart flap like a rag
in your ears as you fell all alone to your
early a.m. death, your last name never
mine, still ripping me apart in the lag
between one childhood crying jag
or another, the word *stepfather*
banned from my vocabulary, clear
insult to your pride, no way to shrug
it off like the birth date, today,
April 25th, you share with Ted
Kooser, whose last line I've stolen away
from his poem about a barbed bedspread
resembling a man fallen asleep on display,
then wind-torn, gone, mere heartbeat in his head.

—Kate Sontag
published in *Verse-Virtual*

"When in the chronicle of wasted time"

I list the ways that I've laid waste to life
I ask if scrolling mail was most to blame,
or reading headlines blazing nations' strife;
or pulling Dames Rocket in its pink flame
from every yard of our backyard's green
and in its stead digging in bulbs—the same
wild hope for springtime blooms I've seen
in ads and fall for every fall—oh shame
to admit what I've fed the local squirrels:
bushels of tulips, armloads of hyacinths,
vanished down the throats of scurrilous
creatures who—insult to injury!—hide
some few for future feasts not in our
backyard but the weedy lots of neighbors.

—Robin Chapman

Poem and Prompt

Caligynephobia

fear of a beautiful woman

I carry who
I used to be
inside my heart,
a sleight of hurt.

The ugly girl
I was at first
lives in this fist,
my hidden trick.

Those nights when hand-
some boys unstick
and exit, quick,
I wake her up

still in my clutch,
enraged. Then: punch.

—Jessica Piazza

We are immediately struck by this poem's unusual title, its one word most likely unfamiliar to many readers. But we recognize the word *phobia* in it, and Piazza quickly provides a definition for this kind of phobia. She gives the phobia to her speaker, a beautiful woman who hides the ugly girl she once was—first inside her heart and then inside her fist. When handsome men run from the beautiful woman she now is, the girl in her fist comes out and gets even.

Piazza, who describes the sonnet form as *chaos in a box*, uses a variation of the form. She gives us fourteen lines but not in iambic pentameter; instead, we have iambic dimeter: four syllables per line, every second one stressed (˘ ' / ˘ '). We have three quatrains and one couplet, a variation of a Shakespearean sonnet; however, while there is rhyme, it does not occur in a pattern. There is only one exact end rhyme: *trick, unstick,* and *quick.* There are several near rhymes: *heart* and *hurt, first* and *fist, clutch* and *punch.*

Assonance adds to the poem's music. Notice the use of words with the long *i* sound: *inside, sleight,* and *nights.* Notice too the use of words with the soft *i* sound: *lives, fist, trick, exit,* and *in.*

Notice how the strategic use of a colon in the last line makes us pause and puts a spotlight on *punch.*

∕ ∕ ∕

For your own poem, first choose a phobia to work with. You might like one of the following:

      Arachnophobia—The fear of spiders
      Cynophobia—The fear of dogs
      Claustrophobia—The fear of small spaces
      Trypophobia—The fear of holes
      Monophobia—The fear of being alone
      Ornithophobia—The fear of birds
      Alektorophobia—The fear of chickens
      Trypanophobia—The fear of needles
      Basiphobia—The fear of falling
      Ailurophobia—The fear of cats

Or find a list of other phobia names by googling.

Or perhaps you have or know of a phobia for which there is no name. Feel free to invent its name and use the phobia for your poem.

Once you've chosen your phobia, internalize it, feel it. Be afraid. How might that phobia affect you or your speaker? Freewrite about your thoughts. Embrace strangeness.

Now mine that rough material for your poem. Try the sonnet form of fourteen lines, three quatrains, one couplet. Challenge yourself to work with iambic feet. You might want to use dimeter as Piazza does, but feel free to try trimeter, tetrameter, or pentameter.

As you revise, attend to the sounds in your poem. Strive for a bit of end rhyme, some near rhymes, and some assonance.

How about a colon?

Sample Poems

Monophobia

fear of being alone

Moving again to a new place,
this time I promise myself
to face what I managed to escape

for years. This time no man in my life
who might or might not stay, not even
a roommate. No longer a wife,

I'll allow only my own voice
to echo from the shower, my plans
for the evening a choice

I'll make at 6 o'clock. Each hour
after I say *No* (not only to men),
how brave I'll feel. What power

to know my tight-held fear might
loosen, the way rhyme can refuse
mere repetition, decide to invite

not a twin but a cousin: If *pure*,
then don't write *cure*. Write
car or *poor*, or even *tear*

(as in tearing up the page where
I'm drafting a poem) or *tears*
(as in filling my eyes when I dare

to enter my flat for the first time
on my own). In a poem
I'm surprised by a rhyme

that's *almost* there, even more
by its being not quite what
I thought I'd hear, but near,

which is better—hearing the turns
as I turn from the door and close it
behind me. A beginning, like learning

to let only the slant sounds in.

—Andrea Hollander

Arachnophobe's Sonnet

Arachnophobia: illogical fear of spiders

On ceiling crack, a black piano key
depressible octet of hairy legs
like fingers playing notes in *lento* crawl
sole melody: my quick and thickening breath.

Both eyelids glued immovable and wide
so sure in darkness it would scale the walls
in undulating rhythm, mount the bed
adagio—with me its only goal.

And should I sleep, like music it would creep
hair-raising whisper 'cross my breast, then face
last kiss before it burrows in my ear
cascading tunnels, past trio of bones

to strike, *da capo*, final minor chord
that resonates unending in my brain.

—Linda Simone

Poem and Prompt

Freeblown

No seams at all, not shaped by any mold
or machine, this bottle two hundred years old,
this pale-blue globe of thinnest glass made with
only a pipe, the glassblower's skill and breath,

and something else, something inside him—yes,
some yearning for light and air, for weightlessness,
desire to hold the afternoon sky, a long
disdain for corners, love of fluid song

as he worked his shift in the factory's heat,
the burns on his hands, his face lacquered with sweat,
the constant dust of his shoes, the shards that lay
beneath each step, their staccato crack all day,

that dark pitched ceiling, the brick furnaces, those
birds so far and faint through the few high windows.

—Elise Hempel

The poet gives us a nonce sonnet, i.e., one that consists of fourteen lines but does not follow the established rhyme scheme or stanza form of either a Shakespearean or Petrarchan sonnet. Hempel's sonnet consists of three quatrains and one closing couplet and has a rhyme scheme of *aabb ccdd eeff gg*. The poet does not slavishly use iambic pentameter, but her lines are ten to twelve syllables.

The poet meditates on a glass blown bottle and then on the glassblower who made the bottle. The first quatrain includes descriptive details about the bottle. The second quatrain includes images pertaining to the glassblower's art and artistic desires.

In the third quatrain the speaker imagines the glassblower at work in the factory.

The subject of this poem is *this bottle two hundred years old*, but notice that there is no verb to complete the sentence. Instead we have a string of modifying phrases. The entire poem consists of a single incomplete sentence that's sustained across the stanzas. This strategy makes the poem flow smoothly and seamlessly from idea to idea and place to place.

✐ ✐ ✐

Every once in a while it's good for our souls to undertake a sonnet. For your own sonnet, choose a single handmade object, perhaps one that represents a lost art or one that continues but is rare. You might, for example, choose a piece of hand-crafted lace, a needlepoint tapestry, or a wood carving, but make it a specific object rather than a general one.

You might want to do a bit of research before you begin drafting. As you read, jot down some details for your poem.

Meditate on your object. Jot down some notes, some descriptive details. Then move to thinking about the maker of the object, again jotting down some notes. Then move to the place where you visualize the object having been made. See it, feel it, hear it. Write down those images.

Now draft your material into a sonnet form of your choosing. Strive to get in a rhyme scheme, but feel free to vary it from the model poem's pattern. You may have strict rhymes or near rhymes—or a mixture.

As you revise, strive for ten to twelve syllables per line. Doing so will compel you to tighten your lines and carefully consider word choices.

Work on the single incomplete sentence structure. This strategy will compel your mind to take leaps and find connections.

Sample Poems

Taming the Pieces: Collage

X-acto knife and extra blades, Mod Podge
for gluing, scissors, ruler, pencil and
eraser, stack of colored papers, wedge
of newsprint, mounting board; a steady hand,
an eye for texture, shape, design—and then
there's patience, willingness to make mistakes,
to alter, reconsider, scrap a plan,
to modify, experiment, unmake,
start over; toiling through a disarray
of colors; cut and move till suddenly
that spark of inspiration, Blessingway
toward realization, epiphany
creating harmony from chaos, cast
in human need for order—whole, at last.

—Scott Wiggerman

Songbird, I Offer You Refuge

for the poet John Haines (1924-2011)

Of cracked, weathered wood, aged by freeze and thaw, hewn
by hand, eye, of plain shape: box, arrow's point, full moon,
assembled with rusted, mismatched screws, crude shelter
for songbird of trill, *jid-it*, hover and flutter;

the poet once scrawled words across the parchment peel
of paper birch trees, cast lines of poems piecemeal
to the sky, carried by ruby-crowned kinglets
migrating north for another season, ringlets

gathered to construct nests of twigs, spider webs, moss,
lined by conifer needles, feathers, down, crisscrossed
with the poet's own craft of homesteading: Amble
the long road north, clear forest, cut trail, haggle

stout roof upon four walls, carve a door facing south;
an ear for sweet bird verse, a page for word of mouth.

—Kersten Christianson

Bonus Prompts: Sonnet

—Jeffrey Bean

1. Shady Character in a Sonnet

Write a sonnet spoken by an invented character who is in some way devious—e.g., a criminal, a liar, a con artist, a cult leader, an art forger. This persona is speaking to an implied listener, a specific other, and is trying to convince that auditor to do something, e.g., get married, invest in a pyramid scheme, steal a car. At some point, perhaps in the usual spot for a volta (turn), let this speaker reveal something surprising that makes him or her more sympathetic. Choose a traditional sonnet form— Shakespearean or Petrarchan. Use iambic pentameter and follow a conventional rhyme scheme, but feel free to utilize slant rhymes, such as consonant rhymes (e.g., spoon/pan) and assonant rhymes (e.g., spoon/fool), in addition to full rhymes (e.g., spoon/June).

2. Animal in an Invented Sonnet

Write a sonnet about an animal. Don't choose a traditional sonnet form—instead, devise your own fourteen-line rhyme scheme. Feel free to use meter or abandon it. Either way, use concrete imagery to bring the animal to life. What colors, smells, textures does it evoke? Try to engage all five senses and use sound and syntax to embody this animal's movements, the noises it makes, how it feels to touch it or look at it or stand in its presence.

3. Borrowing from a Source Sonnet

Find a sonnet you're unfamiliar with and write down the last word of each line. Now write your own sonnet using those fourteen words as the end words of your lines, keeping them in order. Then write another sonnet using the same line-ending words in a different order. Try to make both poems distinct from the original in subject and tone. Give credit to the author of the source sonnet.

XIII. Odd Forms

Not all poems want to do the same pirouette.

—Tami Haaland

Craft Talk: What Does a Poem Want to Be?

—Tami Haaland

Because poetry often comes from a place deeper than the ego, there is a certain mystery about its arrival, and that deeper, less conscious place is at work on many levels. This source is what surprises, what comes up with better rhymes or direction or images than the poet might have been thinking about early in the writing process.

Form too can arrive from this less conscious place, which is probably why the quatrain is the most common form in English. It's familiar and easy to repeat, especially if the poet has little exposure to other patterns. When beginning poets write in quatrains and then struggle with editing because it causes irregularities in the form, I advise them to abandon the quatrains, scrunch the poem together without stanza breaks, and edit away so they can discover the poem's real form later. Not all poems want to do the same pirouette.

A poet becomes agile with form in the same way athletes or musicians or artists become agile—through practice and exercises. Sometimes poets will say they don't write in form, but all poems have some sort of form or pattern, which may include received patterns, open patterns, or invented patterns. In any instance, practice provides the poet with greater capacity to discover what form fits best. A couple weeks writing a sonnet every day, a couple weeks of villanelles, terza rima, rondeau, prose poems, heavily enjambed lines, long lines, short lines, heavy use of white space or any other kind of exploration will allow these patterns to settle into the back of the mind.

The point is not to aim for brilliance but to walk haltingly through the first day or two, and then through the next few days until the form becomes familiar, and then further until language surfaces more swiftly, and the inevitable slack is easier to edit out or transform. This is part of what allows a poem to find its way. A writer might recognize halfway through the writing process or much later, almost as if by accident, that a poem is turning out to be a sonnet, for example, or that it wants to have long lines and substantial stanzas of fifteen lines or more.

Open form, or free verse, always strikes me as a kind of sculpting, like finding the shape inside the stone or, perhaps more accurately, shaping clay. Invention and discovery are part of what happens as the writer works with words to see how they might fall upon the page, where lines can begin and end while allowing the line to maintain its integrity. Enjambment, delay, and white space become part of the rhythm of the poem, and the poet will be actively engaged in experimenting to see how the final piece finds its form—in other words, the form that will compliment the content.

All art incorporates tension, and poetry is no different. While fiction or drama most often include conflict between characters or a character's conflict with self or setting, one way that poetry creates tension is with form and expectation. Let's say a writer is working in a received form, like a sonnet. Tension comes through variation, the poem pushing against the requirements of the form or even against the expectations established in earlier lines. Lockstep iambic pentameter with no surprising language or rhyme, for example, can lull the reader, while variation or unexpected words or phrases can intrigue the reader. Consider Shakespeare's Sonnet 29, how, after ten end-stopped lines, the poet gives us the *lark arising / from sullen earth*, which floats through the end of the line and into the next unlike anything that happened earlier in the poem.

Here are a few tips for developing agility and greater skill in helping the poem discover its form:

1. Practice. Write poems you are not invested in. Five haiku or tanka in the half hour between appointments. A sonnet or sestina, ghazal, triolet, or pantoum until you understand something about the patterns. Don't worry about whether they make sense.

2. Write a poem in a single long stanza, then freely add or edit out lines. When you feel that you're coming close to what the poem wants to say, consider how it looks and behaves on the page.

3. Count lines and divide a poem into three-line stanzas, then four-line and so on. Read through each version. See what happens to the poem as a result of one arrangement or another. See which pattern enhances or contributes to the content.

4. Alternatively, look for places where a poem shifts in tone or image, point of view, or idea. Then divide into irregular stanzas with those shifts as your guide.

5. Count syllables per line and see how your poem is trending. If you find a range in the first few lines, try working within that range in the following lines.

6. Try odd numbers of lines per stanza. An odd number of lines per stanza creates asymmetry. If quatrains are commonplace, then a five-line stanza creates delay, a kind of jazzy lengthening that can add to a reader's anticipation.

7. Recognize when the poem's form surprises you. Recognize how it seems to be landing on the page and trust that shape.

8. Avoid rigidity. A poem forced into a particular shape against its will inevitably shows the scars.

None of this is to advocate for one kind of form or another. Every culture has certain inherited patterns, and most poets are engaged in the process of invention and discovery, but above all, the poet works in service to the poem.

Poem and Prompt

Triolets on a Dune Shack

> *. . . snuggled in between two small glassy dunes, facing the ocean.*
> —Lester Walker, *The Tiny Book of Tiny Houses*

1.

We make love only once in the dune shack.
Our reflections stroke each other in the mirrors,
The pot-bellied stove by the bunk bed glowing black.
We make love only once in the dune shack.
Atlantic winds rattle the French doors,
Sand drifts against us on the bolsters.
We make love only once in the dune shack.
Our reflections stroke each other in the mirrors.

2.

Let's say: we never made love in the dune shack—
We kissed and walked away, dunes glassy around us.
We gazed out to sea, we never looked back.
We tell ourselves: we never made love in the dune shack.
We stopped short, where the weathered driftwood found us,
And turned away in the lee of the dune grass.
We never made love, we say, in the dune shack.
We kissed and walked away, the dunes glassy around us.

—Carolyne Wright

The poet gives us not just a single triolet but a double triolet. The triolet has a prescribed rhyme scheme and use of repetition. The pattern may confound you initially, but don't let it. It's really pretty straightforward. The triolet consists of eight lines. Only five of the lines are original—the remaining three are repeated lines.

Here's the pattern:

1	A	first line
2	B	second line
3	a	Rhymes with 1st line
4	A	repetition of 1st line
5	a	Rhymes with 1st line
6	b	Rhymes with 2nd line
7	A	repetition of 1st line
8	B	repetition of 2nd line

You can see from the pattern that a triolet consists of only two rhymes indicated by A and B. The capitalized letters indicate a repeated line; the lower case letters indicate a rhyme.

Now let's look at Wright's poem. Wright precedes her poem with an epigraph, a quotation drawn from a book. An epigraph should relate to the poem that follows and should act as a lens through which the poem is read. It is better not to have an epigraph than to have one that is irrelevant or pretentious or too long.

Because of its form, the triolet lends itself to trivial subjects, but the greater challenge is to use it with a significant topic, a challenge Wright takes on successfully. You can see in this poem that lines 1 and 2 are especially important as they get repeated. Those lines must bear repeating. Notice that Wright varies her repeated lines a bit by adding or reversing a few words.

You might notice also that Wright takes one liberty with the pattern: line 5 should be an *a* rhyme but she makes it a *b* rhyme and does so in both triolets. But you might want to just stick with the pattern.

Notice that the second triolet is the opposite of the first. The first is about making love; the second is about not making love.

🖋 🖋 🖋

Now for your own double triolet. You may find it helpful to put the numbers and letters down the left side of your page before you begin your triolet.

Like Wright you might draw inspiration from something you've read. So begin by finding a good quotation to use as your epigraph, perhaps something you read in a book or heard in the news. Let that inspire your poem. Remember, though, that an epigraph is an option, not a requirement.

Select a topic of some importance, e.g., a kiss of betrayal, your child's first broken heart, a devastating storm, the death of your beloved dog.

Then begin with your first line. You may find it helpful to add that line in the spaces for lines 4 and 7.

Now write line 2 and also add it in the line 8 space.

Complete your first triolet.

For your second triolet, consider the opposite of the first.

Again, fill in the pattern.

Revise out unnecessary words. Consider your punctuation and how varying it might alter meaning. Perhaps add a colon or a dash somewhere to shake up things a bit.

Sample Poems

You Set a Fun Table, Betsy

The first to Guacamole in your wheelchair,
you drink a prickly pear margarita with salt
and straw, with cheers for the mañanas we'll share.

The first to Guacamole in your wheelchair,
your muscles falter, but your backbone's ironware
ready to pack up and go whenever I call.

The first to Guacamole in your wheelchair
I drink a margarita with you, no need for salt.

*

Your last time to Guacamole in your wheelchair
you spooned a cut-up tamale with chili sauce.
Though Death's on life's menu, we're never prepared,

and your last time to Guacamole in your wheelchair
your wit was still cooking, more spitfire to spare.
Now at a Mexican restaurant, I pause

for you, Betsy, the first to Guacamole in your wheelchair,
blowing off steam. One hot tamale with chili sauce.

—Denise Utt

After the Call from the Animal Welfare Office:
A Triple Triolet

We find cats in the cupboards, the tub, and under the sink.
They crouch and huddle, with flattened ears, their eyes round.
Our eyes water over masks that can't keep out the stink.
We find cats in the cupboards, the table, and under the sink.
They have lived in this air with little food and nothing to drink.
When we touch them, they roll like pill bugs and utter no sound.
We find cats in the bed frame, the drawers, and under the sink.
They crouch and huddle, with flattened ears, their mouths round.

We crouch and huddle, as we coo and sing, our mouths round
behind our masks when we pull cats from under the leaky sink.
We put them into carriers and snap the latch; they utter no sound.
In filth, these cats pray their cat prayers for something to drink.
We scoop cats from the cupboards, counters, and under the sink.
Our eyes water. Think of the pink tongues, their noses in this stink.
They crouch and huddle in the stacked carriers, their eyes round.
We found cats in the cupboards, the tub, and under the sink.

A family lived with cats in the cupboards, the tub, under the sink.
Their kids crouched and huddled with 133 cats, their eyes round.
Their eyes watered over homework and prayers in this foul stink.
They found cats under their beds, on the table, and under the sink.
They have breathed in this air with little food and soda to drink.
When the cats touched them, they cuddled and made the sound
of comfort, thinking this was love, forgetting more cats under one sink,
cats that crouch and huddle, with flattened ears, their mouths round.

—Luanne Castle

Poem and Prompt

Balloon Shop

> *Tell me what you know about dreaming.*
> —Kid Cudi

Nearly as often as not
when I walk by the balloon shop on your block
   I have this drawn-out thought
of all the balloons it has in stock
   inflated to fullness, knotted and taut.

Yellow and green and blue,
they bubble from the shop into the sky,
   cluster in air for a moment or two
above buildings but not too high
   and glow where the sun shines through.

A balloon for every dream in town,
I think to myself on the street below.
   (The same few dreams abound, abound.)
Up and out and apart they go;
   Off they drift without a sound.

Do not come down! Do not come down!
A time will come, they won't obey.
   They'll drop alone on muddy grounds,
while above the city silently
   a new balloon cloud mounts.

—Matthew Yeager

Yeager begins with an epigraph which shoves the poem into action and provides the poet with the subject of dreaming. The first-person speaker imagines that balloons of many colors in a nearby balloon shop blow up to fullness and float into the sky.

Each balloon represents the dream of one dreamer in town, but many of the dreams are the same. In time, the speaker believes, the balloons will fall down, but they will be replaced by new balloons, new dreams.

Notice the form of the poem. This form is called a *quintilla*. Each stanza has five lines. There may be any number of stanzas. By definition the poem should consist of octosyllabic lines, i.e., eight syllables per line, but this is a rule not followed by the poet.

The number of rhymes is limited to two, a rule the poet follows.

There are several rhyme scheme options for a quintilla; Yeager has chosen *ababa*. The quintilla may not end with a rhyming couplet and this one doesn't.

The limitation to only two rhymes means that those sounds must be carefully chosen. Notice that Yeager uses both perfect and near rhymes, thus giving himself more flexibility with the rhyming words.

The poet also adds a visual appeal to the poem by alternating indented lines with lines flush to the left margin.

🖋 🖋 🖋

Let's try a quintilla. For your epigraph, find a sentence or two from another source. Your epigraph should suggest your poem's subject and serve as a lens through which the poem may be read.

Keeping the epigraph in mind, do a wild freewriting on your subject. Follow where the epigraph leads you.

When you've fully exploited the subject, go back through what you've generated and wrestle it into a quintilla. Break the material into five-line stanzas. Notice the end sounds. Now impose the *ababa* rhyme scheme on your draft. This will necessitate some word changes. Let that be a challenge you happily undertake. Remember that you can use both perfect and near rhymes. Remember too that you may, if you like, rearrange the rhyme scheme as long as you stick to just two rhymes.

In subsequent drafts, refine and tighten your lines. Get in some colors for visual imagery. If you like, work on getting octosyllabic lines.

When the poem feels close to finished, work on the format. You might choose the same pattern of alternating indented lines with those flush to the margin, but the choice is up to you.

Sample Poems

The Cry of Coral

Have you ever heard the cry of coral?
It is the tiniest of sounds
Hardly audible amid the ocean's boil
And waves hissing on the sand
Shifting stones into a shining pile.

A blink of light from mother-of-pearl
Or from an opal on your lover's hand
Is louder than the staghorn's wail
Drowns out the weeping of the sea-fan
As one whisper in an Atlantic gale.

On the palm-fringed shore of some isle
Castaways walk their endless rounds
Wondering why the reefs look so pale.
Sailors may yet become unstranded
Coral cannot escape when oceans boil.

Have you ever heard the cry of coral?
Extinction's whisper at the edge of land?
Seen what the beachmongers have for sale?
Jewels stripped from a skeleton crown
Fragments washed up, dead-white and sterile.

—Tiel Aisha Ansari

Possibility

Would you pour concrete into your own wounds?
—Amy Leach

Beethoven poured almond oil
into his ears to stop the creep
of hard silence. To no avail.
Stopper your ears with wax to sleep
with someone who snores. *Voilá!*

you will hear only what crosses
the corpus callosum, the knocks
of knees, the buzz of albatrosses
lost in fog, how the tipsy clocks
hiccup and burble like faucets

that don't shut off, whole symphonies
of storm and drought. Ocean-going
tankers haul sand with equanimity
back through time, west to east, slowing
for locks, dams, the indignity

of being weighed. Wounds in the earth's
surface there make possible dream
homes elsewhere. It takes more structure
than you'd guess to keep wet concrete
from escaping. Such a rupture

is a wound that cannot be cured.
Let openings be passages
to what is possible, tender
bodies and tough, for messages—
no matter how strange—to be heard.

—Athena Kildegaard

Poem and Prompt

You Call with the Diagnosis

Remember the mare,
Mama? Out by the windmill,
foaling? Nothing more

you could do, but still,
you fought. Remember the way
you held her? *Be still,*

you said. The soft gray
of her coat was dark with sweat.
Remember? A ray

lanced the clouds. The wheat
filled its head with easy light.
Remember, you whet

her faint appetite
with an apple slice, then gave
her placenta, bite

by bite. She was saved.
Which am I? Who can be brave?

—J.P. Grasser

The poet precedes the poem with a functional title that lets us know this will be a poem of direct address and it will relay some kind of diagnosis to the speaker. The title immediately creates tension and arouses our curiosity.

The poem itself begins with a question, one of six scattered throughout the poem. This question identifies the auditor, the *you*, as the speaker's mother. She is asked to remember the mare. Using metonymy, the poet then lets the mare stand in for the mother as he closely associates the mare with his mother.

Descriptive details of the earlier recalled scene are used sparingly and strategically. We get the setting—a windmill, a horse foaling, the mother holding the mare, the soft gray of the mare's coat darkened with sweat, the apple slice, and the placenta. Sketching in the scene with a light touch, the poet spotlights what we are meant to see.

Look carefully at the form of Grasser's poem. It's a hybrid poem, one which combines elements of two different forms. There's terza rima here, i.e., three-line stanzas with an interwoven rhyme scheme: *aba bcb cdc, ded, efe,* and a closing couplet of *ff*.

But there's also a haiku hidden in each stanza. Count syllables and you'll find that each stanza equals seventeen syllables.

Pay attention to the end rhymes. Although the poet follows the rhyme scheme of terza rima, he uses straight rhymes (*gray* and *ray*) and slant rhymes (*mare* and *more*), as well as a repeated rhyming word with a different meaning when used a second time (see stanza 2's use of *still*).

✐ ✐ ✐

For your own hybrid poem, first get an auditor in mind. This will be the person to whom you'll be speaking. Give this person a serious problem. We all know such a person, but feel free to use invention.

Begin your draft with a question directed to your auditor. Quickly introduce the metonymy, the thing that is going to stand in for the person addressed. This is difficult. You might want to save it for a later draft.

Once you have your question and your direct address, freewrite your way into the poem. Get in some more questions. Work in some descriptive details but keep them sparse so that they'll take on more importance. When you get to what feels like close to an end, ask yourself a question. Then ask your audience a question.

Now take this freewriting and break it into three-line stanzas. Impose the terza rima form on your freewriting. This will require a careful consideration of your word choices and some changes. Take this as a challenge and be energized by it!

Now aim for the haiku element, giving each stanza seventeen syllables. This is another challenge for you. Embrace it!

Did you like your poem better without the imposition of the form? Feel free to return to the earlier version. Maybe you'll end up with two versions of the same poem. But do try the form. It will be good for your poetic soul.

Commentary: We Hybrid Animals

—J.P. Grasser

Perhaps the most human desire to stem from our flirtations with Reason is that inexhaustible, duplicitous urge to impose order on chaos and chaos on order. When the midnight alleyway roars with silence, we make noise. When the crowded subway car gets too loud, we switch on our noise-canceling headphones. Canoeing on a choppy lake, we pray the wind lets up. If ever we come to the edge of still waters, forced at last to face ourselves, we toss in a pebble or two, and so disturb our images into impressionism, abstraction, the outline of a thought or a shape of an idea. What I mean is, whether by Instinct or Reason or both, we intuit the limits of our senses. We know the *real* is eternally suspect, and we know our imaginations to be the place the world truly inhabits, which is terrifying. As the philosophers would have it, we hybrid animals are forever caught between *being* and *becoming*, along with all the presence and absence that inevitably entails.

The hybrid form I've developed, as displayed in "You Call with the Diagnosis"—Haiku stanza in a Terza Rima scheme—looks to both balance and acknowledge these competing impulses. Of course, the pure numbers game works out nicely, and seems a natural pairing—after all, both forms require the tercet—but more than the arithmetic, for me, were the pesky theoretical underpinnings. Haiku is a form of stark presence, a highly wrought thing that approaches *stillness, staying.* If you've ever spent a hot day digging in a garden, or chopped carrots and celery for hours, or sat at the potter's wheel and felt the clay smooth between your pinch all at once, you've lived a haiku: that briefest of moments when your mind goes blank, your pores all open, and your hairs stand on end. Suddenly there's nothing but body, animal sense, image, presence, and for a second, it's as though all Reason has flooded from you. If you've ever learned to ride a bicycle, or built a bridge out of toothpicks and gumdrops, or thrown a ringer in a game of horseshoes, you've felt the forward momentum of human ambition, architecture, industry, mastery, the propulsive logic for which Dante's schema was perfectly engineered. Simply put, Haiku demands presence, being, circumscription; Terza Rima implies perpetuation, change, continuance. The trouble is, as with most of this living business, both impulses are deeply, deeply human.

As for credit where credit's due, Richard Wilbur's "A Measuring Worm" comes closest to serving as a model for the form. In it, Wilbur constructs five Haiku stanzas with an envelope scheme (*ABA//CDC* and so on), so as to mirror his vermicular subject's scrunching-then-extenuating gait. While Wilbur's rhyming impulse seems to have been more mimetic than purely metaphysical, both forms, I think, strive to apprehend the same great unchanging mysteries—How is it we can both *be* and *become*? How can presence and absence not only coexist, but co-depend, as surely they do? And how, at last, can we represent that whole mess of paradox in a single poetic structure? My own hybrid form in "You Call with the Diagnosis" is a container to hold these opposites and one in which, I hope, the opposites hold.

Sample Poems

The Scan Shows Hydrocephalus

And what did water
mean to us, before? Cool creek
where we led the horse

to drink. Stillness near
green pasture. Penny-plinked well,
spigot and bucket,

summer thunderstorm.
Saturdays after supper
you washed and I dried,

radio playing
AM twang and country swing—
remember those songs?

We rhinestoned the night,
our harmonies clear and close
as bright Opry stars.

Back then did we see
how singing is like swimming?
Love, you once saved me

drowning. I ask you
now, can either of us say
still we like the rain?

—Kory Wells

Across the Great Divide

What were you trying to tell me—to help me learn,
Dad? That time fifty years ago
when you made me watch in Uncle's barn?

The cow stood in that strange, hump-backed way—
she was trying to calve, but the calf was breach.
I wanted to go.   I wanted to stay.

In low light I could see the whites of her rolled eyes.
What was your purpose as you held me there?
Uncle reached into her—up to his elbows—tried

to turn the calf. To my young eyes it looked like pain,
and cruel. Uncle pulled with what?—I don't remember—
his hands or a rope or a slippery chain.

The cow bawled and lurched, Uncle heaved
on the calf's legs, man and cow scrambling in the straw.
By then I couldn't stop looking, didn't want to leave.

Then something gave inside the cow—
a flow of blood and other fluids
as the calf slipped out in a slow

rush and tumble of long legs and damp fur.
Uncle scrubbed the calf with straw. It lifted its head,
searching, the cow turned with a bovine murmur.

Uncle grinned. And Dad, what made your grip
on my shoulders suddenly feel more like a hug?
Surprised, I watched an unexpected tear slip

down your cheek too as we gazed in awe—
blurred—through salt and dust and blood—
at what was born that day in the straw.

You didn't need words.
Who could look away?

—Janet Ruth

Bonus Prompts: Invented Forms

—Allison Joseph

1. The Sweetelle

Write a sweetelle about a holiday that was made special because it was ruined or it was wonderful. Your poem should have ten lines, fourteen syllables per line, and a refrain line at lines 1, 5, and 10. The poem can have a rhyme scheme if you wish, but it is not required. The lines can be metered or syllabic.

2. The Sevenelle

Write a sevenelle about a favorite food or one you loathe. The sevenelle is a seven-line poem with a variable syllable count per line and a rhyme scheme. Follow this pattern:

First line	seven syllables	a
Second line	six syllables	b
Third line	five syllables	c
Fourth line	four syllables	b
Fifth line	five syllables	c
Sixth line	six syllables	b
Seventh line	seven syllables	a

3. The Reverselle

Write a reverselle about a recurring dream, that is, one you've had multiple times. This form lends itself to subjects that have an element of repetition. The reverselle has sixteen lines and a rhyme scheme of *abab cdcd dcdc baba*. The first eight lines are two quatrains. At line 9, duplicate line 8, then repeat lines 1-7 but in reverse order.

Contributors

Tiel Aisha Ansari is the author of several collections, most recently *The Day of My First Driving Lesson*, which received the 2020 Poetry Box chapbook prize, and *Dervish Lions* (Fernwood Press). She hosts the Wider Window Poetry show on KBOO Community Radio.

Pam Baggett is the author of *Wild Horses* (Main Street Rag, 2018). Her awards include a 2019-20 Fellowship in Literature from the North Carolina Arts Council. Her poems have appeared in *Nimrod, Crab Orchard Review*, and *Tar River Poetry*, and in such anthologies as *The Southern Poetry Anthology* and *The Book of Donuts*.

KB Ballentine is the author of seven collections, most recently *Edge of the Echo* (Iris Press, 2021). Her poems have appeared in *Crab Orchard Review, Haight-Ashbury Literary Journal*, and elsewhere, and in such anthologies as *Pandemic Evolution* and *In Plein Air*.

Ellen Bass is the author of four poetry collections, most recently *Indigo* (Copper Canyon, 2020). Her poems have appeared in *The New Yorker, American Poetry Review*, and elsewhere. Her awards include a 2021 Guggenheim Fellowship, an NEA Fellowship, and three Pushcart Prizes. She teaches in the MFA writing program at Pacific University.

Jeffrey Bean is the author of two books of poetry, most recently *Woman Putting on Pearls,* which won the 2016 Red Mountain Prize for Poetry. His poems have appeared in *The Southern Review, The Antioch Review, The Missouri Review, Verse Daily*, and elsewhere. He is Professor of English/Creative Writing at Central Michigan University.

Jan Beatty is the author of six books, most recently *The Body Wars* (University of Pittsburgh Press, 2020). Her earlier book, *Jackknife: New and Selected Poems*, won the 2018 Paterson Prize. She directs creative writing at Carlow University and is Distinguished Writer-in-Residence of the MFA program.

Nina Bennett is the author of three collections, most recently *The House of Yearning* (Kelsay Books, 2018). Her poetry has appeared in *I-70 Review, Gargoyle*, and the *Yale Journal for Humanities in Medicine*. She is a contributing editor for *The Broadkill Review*.

Libby Bernardin is the author of *Stones Ripe for Sowing* (Press 53, 2018) and two chapbooks. She has published poems in *Asheville Poetry Review, Southern Poetry Review*, and elsewhere. She has won awards from the Poetry Society of South Carolina and the North Carolina Poetry Society.

George Bilgere is the author of six books of poetry, most recently *Blood Pages* (University of Pittsburgh Press, 2018). He has received a Pushcart Prize, an NEA grant, the May Swenson Poetry Award, the Cleveland Arts Prize, and a Fullbright Fellowship. He teaches at John Carroll University in Cleveland, Ohio.

Nancy Susanna Breen has published poetry in the anthology *Moving Images: Poetry Inspired by Film* and in the online *Global Poemic*. Her latest chapbook, *Closing My Father's Mouth* (New Dawn Unlimited), won the 2020 Morris Memorial Chapbook Award.

Traci Brimhall is the author of four collections of poetry, most recently *Come the Slumberless to the Land of Nod* (Copper Canyon Press, 2020). Her poems have appeared in *The New Yorker, Poetry*, and *Best American Poetry 2013* and *2014*. The recipient of an NEA Fellowship, she is Director of Creative Writing at Kansas State University.

Ronda Piszk Broatch is the author of *Lake of Fallen Constellations* (MoonPath, 2015). She is the recipient of an Artist Trust GAP Grant. Her journal publications include *Blackbird, Sycamore Review, Missouri Review*, and Public Radio KUOW's *All Things Considered*.

Jayne Brown is the author of *My First Real Tree* (FootHills, 2005). Her poems have appeared in such journals as *Blueline, Cider Press Review*, and *Alligator Juniper*. From 2019-2021 she served as the Poet Laureate for Berks County, Pennsylvania.

Nicole Callihan is the author of *SuperLoop* (Sock Monkey, 2014) and the chapbooks, *The Deeply Flawed Human* (2016) and *Downtown* (2017). Her work has appeared in *Tin House, Sixth Finch,* and the *American Poetry Review*, and as a *Poem-a-Day* selection.

Lauren Camp is the author of five poetry collections, most recently *Took House* (Tupelo Press, 2020). *One Hundred Hungers* (Tupelo Press, 2016) won the Dorset Prize. Her poems have appeared in such journals as *Pleiades, Poet Lore*, and *Beloit Poetry Journal*. Her honors include a Black Earth Institute Fellowship.

Luanne Castle is the author of *Doll God*, winner of the 2015 New Mexico-Arizona Book Award. She has been a Fellow at the Center for Ideas and Society at the University of California, Riverside. Her work has appeared in *Copper Nickel, American Journal of Poetry*, and *Pleiades*.

Robin Rosen Chang is the author of *The Curator's Notes* (Terrapin Books, 2021). Her poems have appeared in *Michigan Quarterly Review, The Journal, Diode,* and elsewhere. She teaches English as a Second Language at Kean University in New Jersey.

Robin Chapman is the author of ten books of poetry, most recently *The Only Home We Know* (Tebot Bach, 2019), winner of a Wisconsin Library Association's Outstanding Poetry Book award. Her other awards include the Helen Howe Poetry Prize.

Kersten Christianson is the author of *Curating the House of Nostalgia* (Sheila-Na-Gig, 2020). She also authored the chapbook, *What Caught Raven's Eye* (Petroglyph, 2018). She is poetry editor of the journal *Alaska Women Speak* and lives in Alaska.

Patricia Clark is the author of six poetry books, most recently *Self-Portrait with a Million Dollars* (Terrapin, 2020), and three chapbooks. She taught for thirty years in the Writing Department at Grand Valley State University in Michigan and was the university's Poet-in-Residence.

Cathy Colman is the author of three books of poetry, most recently *Time Crunch* (What Books, 2019). Her first book, *Borrowed Dress,* won the Felix Pollak Prize. Her poetry has appeared in *Ploughshares, The Gettysburg Review, Prairie Schooner,* and elsewhere.

Gail Comorat is the author of *Phases of the Moon* (FLP) and a collaborating poet for *Walking the Sunken Boards* (Pond Road). She is a founding member of Rehoboth Beach Writers Guild and an editor of *Quartet.* Her work has appeared in *Gargoyle, Grist,* and *Mudfish.*

Geraldine Connolly is the author of four poetry collections, most recently *Aileron* (Terrapin Books, 2018). She has taught at the Writer's Center in Maryland, The Chautauqua Institution, and the University of Arizona Poetry Center. She has received fellowships from the NEA, the Maryland Arts Council, and Bread Loaf Writers' Conference.

Beth Copeland is the author of three poetry books, most recently *Blue Honey,* recipient of the 2017 Dogfish Head Poetry Prize. She owns and operates Tiny Cabin, Big Ideas, a retreat for writers in the Blue Ridge Mountains of North Carolina.

Jane Mary Curran is the author of *Indiana Girl: Poems* (Gridley Fires Books, 2019), and *Midwives of the Spirit: Thoughts on Caregiving* (2002). She is retired from a professorship in piano and a second career as a hospice chaplain and spiritual director.

Jessica de Koninck is the author of *Cutting Room* (Terrapin, 2016). Her poems have appeared in such journals as *Tiferet, Valparaiso Poetry Review*, and *Eclectica*, and have been featured in *The Writer's Almanac* and *Verse Daily*. A retired attorney, she teaches at Saint Peter's University.

Maureen Doallas is the author of *Neruda's Memoirs: Poems* (T.S. Poetry, 2011). Her poems appear in *Every Day Poems* and *Rattle Poets Respond*, and in the anthologies *How to Write a Form Poem* and *A Constellation of Kisses*.

Lynn Domina is the author of two collections of poetry, most recently *Framed in Silence* (Main Street Rag, 2011). Her work appears in *The Gettysburg Review, Los Angeles Review*, and *New England Review*. She is Head of the English Department at Northern Michigan University.

Catherine Doty is the author of two collections of poems, most recently *Wonderama* (CavanKerry, 2021). She is the recipient of a fellowship from the NEA, as well as fellowships from The New Jersey State Council on the Arts and the New York Foundation for the Arts.

Caitlin Doyle's work has appeared in *The Guardian, The Atlantic, The Yale Review*, and elsewhere. She has received fellowships from Yaddo, the MacDowell Colony, the James Merrill House, and the Bread Loaf Writers' Conference. She is Visiting Assistant Professor of English and Writer-in-Residence at Washington & Jefferson College.

George Drew is the author of nine poetry collections, most recently *Drumming Armageddon* (Madville, 2020). His earlier books include *The View from Jackass Hill* (Texas Review Press), winner of the 2010 X.J. Kennedy Poetry Prize.

Camille Dungy is the author of four collections of poetry, most recently *Trophic Cascade* (Wesleyan, 2017), winner of the Colorado Book Award. She is also the author of *Guidebook to Relative Strangers: Journeys into Race, Motherhood, and History*. Her honors include a Guggenheim Fellowship, an American Book Award, and NEA Fellowships.

Dara Yen Elerath is the author of *Dark Braid*, which won the 2019 John Ciardi Prize for Poetry from BkMk Press. Her work appears in such journals as *The American Poetry Review, AGNI*, and *Plume*. She is a graduate of the Institute of American Indian Arts MFA program.

Melanie Figg is the author of *Trace* (New Rivers, 2019). She has won grants from the NEA and the Maryland State Arts Council. Her work has appeared in such journals as *The Rumpus, Nimrod*, and *The Iowa Review*. She teaches writing and offers women's writing retreats.

Robert Fillman is the author of the chapbook, *November Weather Spell* (Main Street Rag, 2019). His poems have appeared in such journals as *Sugar House Review, Tar River Poetry*, and *Valparaiso Poetry Review*. He is an Assistant Professor of English at Kutztown University.

Ann Fisher-Wirth's sixth book of poems is *The Bones of Winter Birds* (Terrapin Books, 2019). A senior fellow of the Black Earth Institute, she is the recipient of senior Fulbrights to Switzerland and Sweden, two MAC Poetry Fellowships, and an MS Institute of Arts and Letters Poetry Prize. She teaches at the University of Mississippi.

Annie Finch is the author of six books of poetry, most recently *Spells: New and Selected Poems* (Wesleyan, 2013). Her poetry has been published in *Poetry, Paris Review, The New York Times*, and elsewhere. Among her books on poetics are *The Body of Poetry: Essays on Women, Form, and the Poetic Self* and *A Poet's Craft*.

Emily Franklin is the author of *Tell Me How You Got Here* (Terrapin Books, 2021). She is also the author of numerous novels and a cookbook. Her writing has appeared in *The New York Times, Guernica*, and *New Ohio Review*, and has been featured on NPR.

Jennifer Franklin is the author of three full-length collections, most recently *If Some God Shakes Your House* (Four Way Books, 2023). Her work has been published in *American Poetry Review, Gettysburg Review, Prairie Schooner*, and elsewhere. She is the Program Director of the Hudson Valley Writers Center.

Joy Gaines-Friedler is the author of three poetry books, most recently *Capture Theory* (Kelsay Books, 2018). Her work has appeared in *New York Quarterly, San Pedro River Review, Rattle*, and elsewhere. Her awards include The Litchfield Review Poetry Prize and The Marjorie J. Wilson Award.

Kate Gaskin is the author of *Forever War*, winner of the Pamet River Prize (YesYes Books, 2020). Her poems have appeared in such journals as *Pleiades, Alaska Quarterly Review*, and *The Southern Review*. Her awards include a scholarship from the Sewanee Writers' Conference and a fellowship from the Vermont Studio Center.

Deborah Gerrish is author of three collections of poems, most recently *Light in Light* (Resource Publications, 2017). Her poems have appeared in *Lips, Paterson Literary Review*, and *A Constellation of Kisses*. She teaches poetry workshops at Fairleigh Dickinson University.

Holiday Goldfarb has received awards from the Deane Wagner Poetry Contest and the 2017 Bi-State Metro Arts in Transit. Her work has appeared in *Entropy* and *Ponder Review*. She is a past Associate Editor of the *Lindenwood Review*.

David Graham has published three books of poetry, most recently *The Honey of Earth* (Terrapin Books, 2019). He co-edited the anthologies *Local News* and *After Confession*. His poems and essays have appeared in numerous journals and anthologies, and have been featured on *Poetry Daily* and *The Writer's Almanac*.

J.P. Grasser is a former Wallace Stegner Fellow and a current PhD candidate at the University of Utah, where he edited *Quarterly West*. He is Associate Editor for *32 Poems*. His poems have appeared in *Poem-a-Day, Diagram, Narrative Magazine,* and *Gulf Coast*.

Jesse Graves is the author of four collections of poetry, most recently *Merciful Days* (Mercer, 2020). He received the 2014 Philip H. Freund Prize and the 2015 James Still Award. He is Professor of English and Poet-in-Residence at East Tennessee State University.

Lucy Griffith is the author of *We Make a Tiny Herd* (Main Street Rag, 2019), winner of the Wrangler Prize for Poetry as well as the Willa Literary Award for Poetry. Recipient of Bread Loaf's Returning Contributor Scholarship in Poetry, she lives on a ranch in Texas.

Tami Haaland, Montana's Poet Laureate from 2013 to 2015, received a MAC Artist Innovation Award. She is the author of three poetry collections, most recently *What Does Not Return* (Lost Horse Press, 2018). Her poems have been featured on *The Slowdown, The Writer's Almanac, Verse Daily,* and *American Life in Poetry*.

Jared Harél is the author of *Go Because I Love You* (Diode Editions, 2018). His awards include the Stanley Kunitz Memorial Prize, the William Matthews Poetry Prize, and two Individual Artist Grants from Queens Council on the Arts. His poems have appeared in such journals as *Ploughshares, The Southern Review,* and *The Threepenny Review*.

Lois Marie Harrod is the author of numerous collections, most recently the chapbook *Spat* (FLP, 2021). Her poems have appeared in such journals as *American Poetry Review, Off the Coast,* and *Zone 3*. She has received three poetry fellowships from the New Jersey State Council on the Arts.

Penny Harter's most recent collection is *Still-Water Days* (Kelsay, 2021) Her work has appeared in *Persimmon Tree, Rattle,* and *Tiferet,* as well as in Ted Kooser's *American Life in Poetry*. Her awards include three fellowships from the New Jersey State Council on the Arts.

Lisa Hase-Jackson is the author of *Flint and Fire* (The Word Works, 2019), winner of the 2019 Hilary Tham Capital Collection Series. Her poems have appeared in *The Midwest Quarterly, Kansas City Voices,* and *The South Carolina Review.* She is editor of the *South 85 Journal* and founding editor of *Zingara Poetry Review.*

Shayla Hawkins is the author of *Carambola* (David Robert Books, 2012). Her poems have appeared in such journals as *Bonsai, Calabash,* and *The Taj Mahal Review,* and in such anthologies as *Chopin with Cherries, Joys of the Table,* and *A Constellation of Kisses.*

Elise Hempel's first book, *Second Rain,* was published by Able Muse Press in 2016. Her poems have appeared in such journals as *Poetry* and *Southern Poetry Review,* and in *Verse Daily, Poetry Daily,* and Ted Kooser's *American Life in Poetry.* She received an Illinois Arts Council Literary Award and the 2016 String Poet Prize.

Andrea Hollander is the author of five poetry collections, most recently *Blue Mistaken for Sky* (Autumn House, 2018). Her awards include the Nicholas Roerich Poetry Prize, two fellowships from the NEA, two Pushcart Prizes, and the 2021 49th Parallel Award in Poetry.

Karen Paul Holmes is the author of two poetry collections, most recently *No Such Thing as Distance* (Terrapin Books, 2018). Her poems have been featured on *The Writer's Almanac* and Tracy K. Smith's *The Slowdown.* Her publications include *Prairie Schooner, Pedestal,* and *Valparaiso Poetry Review.*

Jenny Hubbard has published poems in *The Crafty Poet* and *The Practicing Poet,* both from Terrapin Books. Her first novel, *Paper Covers Rock* (Delacorte, 2012), was a finalist for the ALA's Morris Award; her second novel, *And We Stay,* earned a Printz Honor Award.

Allison Joseph is the author of several collections, including *Confessions of a Barefaced Woman* (Red Hen, 2018), a finalist for the NAACP Image Award in Poetry. She teaches at Southern Illinois University, is editor of *Crab Orchard Review,* and directs the Writers in Common Conference.

W. Todd Kaneko is the author of two poetry books, most recently *This Is How the Bone Sings* (Black Lawrence, 2020). His poems have appeared in *Massachusetts Review, Alaska Quarterly Review,* and *Poetry,* and have been featured on *Poetry Daily* and *Poem-a-Day.* A Kundiman Fellow, he teaches at Grand Valley State University.

Christen Noel Kauffman's hybrid chapbook, *Notes to a Mother God,* was a 2021 winner of the Paper Nautilus Debut Chapbook Series. Her work has appeared in *A Harp in the Stars: An Anthology of Lyric Essays* (University of Nebraska, 2021), and in such journals as *Nimrod, The Cincinnati Review,* and *The Normal School.*

Meg Kearney is the author of three collections of poetry, most recently *All Morning the Crows* (Word Works, 2021), winner of the 2020 Washington Prize, and three verse novels for teens. Her poetry has been featured on *A Writer's Almanac* and *American Life in Poetry.* She directs the Solstice MFA in Creative Writing Program.

Tina Kelley is the author of four collections, most recently *Rise Wildly* (CavanKerry Press, 2020). She co-authored the non-fiction *Breaking Barriers* and *Almost Home.* Her writing has appeared in *Southwest Review, Prairie Schooner,* and the *Best American Poetry 2009.*

Adele Kenny is the author of several collections of poetry, most recently *Wind Over Stones* (Welcome Rain, 2019). Her awards include two poetry fellowships from the New Jersey State Council on the Arts, a Merton Poetry of the Sacred Award, and a Women of Excellence Award. She is the poetry editor of *Tiferet Journal.*

Jemshed Khan is the author of the chapbook *Speech in an Age of Certainty* (Finishing Line Press). His poems have been published in such journals as *I-70 Review, Chiron Review, Fifth Estate,* and *San Pedro River Review.*

Athena Kildegaard is the author of six books of poetry, most recently *Prairie Midden* (Tinderbox Editions, 2021). She is the co-editor of the anthology *Rocked by the Waters: Poems of Motherhood* (Nodin Press). She teaches at the University of Minnesota Morris, where she is also the director of the honors program.

Kim Klugh's poetry has been published in *Vox Poetica, Global Poemic,* and *I Am Still Waiting* (Silver Birch Press). Her poems have also appeared in *The Practicing Poet* and *The Crafty Poet II,* both from Terrapin Books. She works as an English/writing tutor.

Lynne Knight has published six full-length collections, including *The Persistence of Longing* (Terrapin, 2016). Her work has appeared in such journals as *Beloit Poetry Journal, Georgia Review,* and *Southern Review.* Her awards include a Prix de l'Alliance Française, a PSA Lucille Medwick Memorial Award, a Rattle Poetry Prize, and an NEA grant.

Danusha Laméris is the author of two collections, most recently *Bonfire Opera* (University of Pittsburgh, 2020), winner of the Northern California Book Award. Her work has been published in *The Best American Poetry, The New York Times, Ploughshares*, and elsewhere. She is on the faculty of Pacific University's low residency MFA program.

Lance Larsen has published five poetry collections, most recently *What the Body Knows* (University of Tampa, 2018). His awards include a Pushcart Prize, the Tampa Review Prize, and an NEA Fellowship. He is professor of English at BYU and serves as associate department chair.

Marcia LeBeau's poems and essays have been published in *New Ohio Review, Rattle, Painted Bride Quarterly,* and elsewhere. She is a teaching artist and plays viola in her local symphony. She is founder of The Write Space in NJ, a co-working and literary hub for creative writers.

Diane LeBlanc is the author of four poetry chapbooks and a full-length collection, *The Feast Delayed* (Terrapin Books, 2021). Her work appears in *Bellingham Review, Cimarron Review, Green Mountains Review,* and elsewhere. She is a professor of writing at St. Olaf College.

Ada Limón, a Guggenheim fellow, is the author of five poetry collections, including *The Carrying*, which won the National Book Critics Circle Award for Poetry. She teaches in the Queens University of Charlotte low-residency MFA program.

Denise Low's most recent collection is *Wing* (Red Mountain, 2021). Her memoir, *The Turtle's Beating Heart: One Family's Story of Lenape Survival* (University of Nebraska, 2017), was a Hefner Heitz Award finalist. She served as the Kansas Poet Laureate 2007-09 and founded the creative writing program at Haskell Indian Nations University.

Charlotte Mandel is the author of eleven books of poetry, most recently *Alive and In Use: Poems in the Japanese Form of Haibun* (Kelsay Books, 2019). Her awards include a Lifetime Achievement Award from Brooklyn College, the New Jersey Poets Prize, and two poetry fellowships from the New Jersey State Council on the Arts.

Joan Mazza has worked as a medical microbiologist and psychotherapist. She is the author of six books, including *Dreaming Your Real Self.* Her poetry has appeared in *Prairie Schooner, Poet Lore,* and *The Nation.*

Melanie McCabe is the author of two volumes of poetry, most recently *What the Neighbors Know* (FutureCycle Press, 2014), as well as a memoir. Her work has appeared in *The Washington Post, The Georgia Review, Threepenny Review,* and elsewhere.

Kerrin McCadden is the author of *American Wake* (Black Sparrow, 2021) and *Landscape with Plywood Silhouettes*, winner of the Vermont Book Award and the New Issues Poetry Prize. The recipient of an NEA Fellowship, she is associate poetry editor at Persea Books and associate director of the Conference on Poetry and Teaching at The Frost Place.

Lynn McGee is the author of two poetry collections, most recently *Tracks* (Broadstone Books, 2019), as well as two award-winning chapbooks. Her first children's book, *Starting Over in Sunset Park*, was co-written with Jose Pelauz (Tilbury House, 2021).

Maren O. Mitchell is the author of a nonfiction book, *Beat Chronic Pain: An Insider's Guide*. Her poems have appeared in *The MacGuffin, Poetry East, Tar River Poetry*, and elsewhere. She received the First Place Award for Excellence from the Georgia Poetry Society.

Brad Aaron Modlin is the author of two collections, most recently *Everyone at This Party Has Two Names* (Southeast Missouri State, 2016), which won the Cowles Prize. He is the Reynolds Endowed Chair of Creative Writing at the University of Nebraska Kearney, where he teaches and curates the visiting writers series.

Erin Murphy is the author of eight books of poetry, including *Human Resources* (Salmon, 2021). Her work has appeared in such journals as *The Georgia Review, Southern Poetry Review*, and *North American Review*. Her awards include The Normal School Poetry Prize, the Dorothy Sargent Rosenberg Poetry Prize, and the Foley Poetry Prize.

Peter E. Murphy is the author of two poetry collections, most recently *The Man Who Never Was* (Unsolicited Press, 2018). His poems have appeared in such journals as *Beloit Poetry Journal, Diode*, and *Rattle*. His awards include fellowships from the New Jersey State Council on the Arts. He is the founder of Murphy Writing of Stockton University.

David O'Connell is the author of *Our Best Defense* (Cervena Barva, 2021). His chapbook, *A Better Way to Fall*, was awarded the Philbrick Poetry Award. His poems have appeared in *New Ohio Review, The Cincinnati Review, Copper Nickel*, and elsewhere.

Matthew Olzmann is the author of two collections of poems, most recently *Mezzanines* (Alice James, 2013), winner of the Kundiman Prize. He has received fellowships from Kundiman, the Kresge Arts Foundation, and the Bread Loaf Writers' Conference. He teaches at Dartmouth College and in the MFA Program for Writers at Warren Wilson College.

Dion O'Reilly is the author of *Ghost Dogs* (Terrapin Books, 2020). Her poems appear in such journals as *New Letters, Rattle,* and *The Massachusetts Review.* Her work has also appeared in a number of anthologies, including *A Constellation of Kisses.* She is a member of The Hive Poetry Collective, which produces podcasts and radio shows.

Jessica Piazza is the author of three poetry collections, most recently *Obliterations* (Red Hen, 2016). She cofounded *Bat City Review* and Gold Line Press, and was the 2019 recipient of the Amy Clampitt residency award. She is a writing professor at the University of Southern California and a book club facilitator for Literary Affairs.

Catherine Pierce, Poet Laureate of Mississippi 2021-2025, is the author of four poetry collections, most recently *Danger Days* (Saturnalia, 2020). An NEA Fellow and two-time Pushcart Prize winner, she is Professor of English at Mississippi State University.

Jenna Rindo has had work published in such journals as *Calyx,* the *American Journal of Nursing, Comstock Review, Tampa Review,* and *Bellingham Review.* A former pediatric intensive care nurse, she now teaches English to non-native speakers.

Janet Ruth's first book, *Feathered Dreams* (Mercury HeartLink, 2018) was a finalist for the 2018 NM/AZ Book Awards. She won the 2019 Tucson Festival of Books Literary Award for Poetry for a group of five poems. She is a New Mexico ornithologist whose poems have appeared in *Sin Fronteras, Spiral Orb, Ekphrastic Review,* and elsewhere.

Jennifer Saunders is the author of *Self-Portrait with Housewife* (Tebot Bach, 2019), winner of the Clockwise Chapbook Competition. She is the winner of the 2020 Gregory O'Donoghue International Poetry Prize, and her work has appeared in *The Georgia Review, Grist, Ninth Letter,* and elsewhere. She lives in German-speaking Switzerland.

James Scruton is the author of two collections and five chapbooks, most recently *The Rules* (Green Linden , 2019). His work has appeared in such publications as *North American Review, Poetry East,* and *Poetry.* He is Professor of English and Associate Academic Dean at Bethel University in Tennessee.

Diane Seuss is the author of five poetry collections, most recently *frank: sonnets* (Graywolf Press, 2021). Her earlier book, *Four-Legged Girl* (Graywolf, 2015), was a finalist for the Pulitzer Prize. A 2020 Guggenheim Fellow, she received the John Updike Award from the American Academy of Arts and Letters in 2021.

Rob Shapiro received an MFA from the University of Virginia where he was awarded the Academy of American Poets Prize. His poetry has appeared in *AGNI, The Southern Review,* and *Ecotone*, and has received the Edward Stanley Award from *Prairie Schooner.*

Sean Shearer is the author of the collection, *Red Lemons*, which won the 2019 Akron Poetry Prize. His honors include a Pushcart Prize and a fellowship from the Vermont Studio Center. A former Poe/Faulkner Fellow at the University of Virginia, he is the editor-in-chief of BOAAT Press.

Linda Simone's most recent poetry collection is *The River Will Save Us* (Kelsay Books, 2018). Her other publications include two chapbooks and *Moon: A Poem*, a book for young children. Her poems have appeared on museum sites, public buses, storefront windows, coffee coasters, and menus.

Kate Sontag is coeditor of the essay anthology, *After Confession: Poetry as Autobiography* (Graywolf, 2001). Winner of the Ron H. Bayes Poetry Prize, her work has been published in *Prairie Schooner, Crab Orchard Review*, and *Rattle,* and featured in *Valparaiso Poetry Review.*

Adam Tavel is the author of four books of poetry, including *Sum Ledger* (Measure, 2021). His previous collection, *Catafalque*, won the Richard Wilbur Award (University of Evansville, 2018). He is a professor of English at Wor-Wic Community College, where he also directs the Echoes & Visions Reading Series.

Marilyn L. Taylor, former Poet Laureate of Wisconsin, is the author of six poetry collections, including *Step on a Crack* (Kelsay Books, 2016). Her poems have appeared in such journals as *Poetry, The American Scholar*, and *Measure*. She is a contributing editor for *Third Wednesday* and *Verse-Virtual.*

Betsy Thorne is the author of *Measured Words* (Main Street Rag, 2019). She is a past recipient of prizes from the South Carolina Poetry Initiative and the South Carolina Writers Workshop. Her poems have appeared in *The Squaw Valley Review, Kakalak*, and *Yemassee.*

J. C. Todd is the author of three books of poetry, most recently *Beyond Repair* (2021), a special selection for the 2019 Able Muse Press Book Award. Her honors include the 2016 Rita Dove Poetry Prize and fellowships from the Pew Center for Arts and Heritage and the Pennsylvania Council on the Arts.

Denise Utt's poetry has appeared in the *Bellevue Literary Review, Paterson Literary Review,* and the *Forgotten Women Anthology*. Her lyrics have been recorded in the R&B hit "What I Wouldn't Do (for the Love of You)" and the jazz song "I Don't Want No Happy Songs."

Lisken Van Pelt Dus is the author of *What We're Made Of* (Cherry Grove, 2016). She teaches writing, languages, and martial arts. Her poetry appears in such journals as *Conduit, Pirene's Fountain,* and *Gleam,* and has earned awards from *The Comstock Review* and *Atlanta Review.*

Craig van Rooyen's poems have appeared in *Best New Poets, New Ohio Review, Ploughshares,* and elsewhere. He is a past winner of the Rattle Poetry Prize. Van Rooyen received his MFA in Poetry from Pacific University. He is a judge living in California.

Sara Moore Wagner is the recipient of a 2019 Sustainable Arts Foundation award and the author of the chapbooks *Tumbling After* (Red Bird, 2022) and *Hooked Through* (2017). Her poetry has appeared in such journals as *Beloit Poetry Journal, Rhino,* and *The Cincinnati Review.*

Frank X Walker, the first African American writer to be named Kentucky Poet Laureate, is Professor of English and African American and Africana Studies at the University of Kentucky. He has published eleven collections of poetry, most recently *Masked Man, Black: Pandemic & Protest Poems* (Accents Publishing, 2020).

BJ Ward is the author of four books of poetry, most recently *Jackleg Opera* (North Atlantic, 2013), which received the Paterson Award for Literary Excellence. He is the recipient of a Pushcart Prize and two fellowships from the New Jersey State Council on the Arts. He teaches at Warren County Community College.

Kory Wells is the author of *Sugar Fix* (Terrapin, 2019). Her writing has been featured on *The Slowdown* poetry podcast and appears in the *James Dickey Review, Ruminate, Stirring,* and elsewhere. The former inaugural Poet Laureate of Murfreesboro, Tennessee, she is a mentor with the low-residency program at Middle Tennessee State University.

Bruce E. Whitacre has published work in the *American Journal of Poetry, Buddhist Poetry Review, Cagibi,* and elsewhere. His work has also appeared in the anthology, *I Want to be Loved by You: Poems on Marilyn Monroe* (Milk and Cake, 2022) and in *Brownstone Poets 2020.*

Scott Wiggerman is the author of three books of poetry, most recently *Leaf and Beak: Sonnets* (Purple Flag, 2015). He is the co-editor of several volumes from Dos Gatos Press, including *Wingbeats: Exercises & Practice in Poetry* (I and II). His poems have appeared in *Sin Fronteras, Right Hand Pointing, Anti-Heroin Chic,* and elsewhere.

Shannon K. Winston's debut full-length poetry collection is *The Girl Who Talked to Paintings* (Glass Lyre, 2021). Her poems have appeared in *Crab Creek Review, The Night Heron Barks, RHINO, Rust + Moth*, and elsewhere.

Elizabeth S. Wolf won the 2018 Rattle Chapbook contest for *Did You Know?* She is also the author of a full-length collection, *When Lawyers Wept* (Kelsay Books, 2019). Her poems appear in *Ibbetson Street, Silkworm*, and the *Boston Literary Magazine*.

Carolyne Wright is the author of six poetry books, most recently *This Dream the World: New & Selected Poems* (Lost Horse, 2017). She is also the author of a volume of essays and three volumes by Bengali women poets in translation. Her awards include an NEA Fellowship, 4Culture grants, and a 2020-2021 Fulbright Scholar Award.

Matthew Yeager is the author of *Like That* (Forklift, 2016). His poems have appeared in *American Poetry Review, Poem-a-Day*, and *The Best American Poetry 2005* and *2010*. His honors include the Barthelme Prize in short prose and fellowships to MacDowell and Yaddo. He is co-curator of the KGB Monday Night Poetry Series.

Dean Young is the author of several collections, most recently *Solar Perplexus* (Copper Canyon, 2019). His *Elegy on Toy Piano* (University of Pittsburgh, 2005) was a finalist for the Pulitzer Prize. He has received a Stegner Fellowship, as well as NEA and Guggenheim Fellowships.

Michael T. Young's third collection is *The Infinite Doctrine of Water* (Terrapin, 2018). He is the recipient of a fellowship from the New Jersey State Council on the Arts. His poetry has been featured on *Verse Daily* and *The Writer's Almanac*, and has appeared in such journals as *Cimarron Review, Rattle*, and *Valparaiso Poetry Review*.

Yvonne Zipter is the author of three poetry collections, most recently *Kissing the Long Face of the Greyhound* (Terrapin Books, 2020). She is also the author of two nonfiction books and a Russian historical novel, *Infraction* (Rattling Good Yarns, 2021). She appears in and provided some narration for the documentary film, *A Secret Love*.

Credits

Index

About the Editor

Diane Lockward is the editor of three earlier craft books: *The Practicing Poet: Writing Beyond the Basics* (Terrapin Books, 2018), *The Crafty Poet II: A Portable Workshop* (Terrapin Books, 2016), and *The Crafty Poet: A Portable Workshop* (Terrapin Books, rev. ed., 2016). She is also the author of four poetry books, most recently *The Uneaten Carrots of Atonement* (Wind Publications, 2016). Her awards include the Quentin R. Howard Poetry Prize, a poetry fellowship from the New Jersey State Council on the Arts, and a Woman of Achievement Award. Her poems have been included in such journals as the *Harvard Review, Southern Poetry Review*, and *Prairie Schooner*. Her work has also been featured on *Poetry Daily, Verse Daily, The Writer's Almanac*, and Ted Kooser's *American Life in Poetry*. She is the founder and publisher of Terrapin Books.